I Wrote My Own Ticket to Success

I Wrote My Own Ticket to Success-

Helen Stefanick

1. Decades
2. 1980's
3. Love Story
4. Introspection
5. Memoir

Dedication

This book was not meant to be a love story, but a story of emotions. Everyday people enter and exit our lives. Some leave an imprint; some may wait until tomorrow to reflect upon us. Someday all our paths cross again.

This is a story of the eighties when you danced to music, wild and free. Free spirited days of love, romance and "finding yourself".

We all try to succeed in our own life plan, but to succeed emotionally, is a totally different story.

Acknowledgements

To Jan, my lifelong friend and confidant. Thank you for always being a great listener and adventurer.

To Roman, for being that special person in my life who showed me how to live life today and take the past as a stepping stone carrying the positive. Thank you for your guidance in helping me laugh again.

To my husband, Paul for encouraging me to pursue my dreams.

And finally to my daughter, Ivana for giving me the enthusiasm to live life and write again. You are my life.

Prologue

Growing up Ellen always wondered what would be in store for her life. She loved art and doodled constantly whenever pen in hand, mapping her thoughts and dreams. Growing up in the sixties was a very adventurous time with crazy fads, music and originality. She grew up with her older sister, Julie, in a very "Ozzie and Harriet" type of household. Their parents would usually just smile, and shake their heads with a "what is this world coming to?" expression upon their faces. The seventies came quickly for Ellen's high school years. She did not make friends readily. Instead, she would stand aside and observe as to question whether they would be a "true friend". Until Chuck entered her life. Football quarterback. Her best friend throughout school years, her confidant, and idea- bouncing partner. Boyfriend? No! Best friend. Chuck had Simone. A beautiful classmate that he adored. Ellen always respected her and was glad for their happiness. Someday she wished for that kind of relationship. As the years passed, Chuck and Ellen grew apart, both by distance and hectic lives. Ellen moved from home pursuing a career in art. However, the jobsites never panned out and in the midst of it all landed a job in the medical profession to support herself. She found a new niche that was rewarding. New friends, new apartment. Wow!! As the seventies rolled in, the nightclub scene ruled. Disco days !! Ellen and her friends would frequent night clubs every weekend to wind down from the work week. And thus, Ellen met Peter. A handsome, six foot two, dark haired, brown eyed wonder. The two were inseparable, especially on weekends. They became the infamous " Peter and Ellen."

I Wrote My Own Ticket to Success

Chapter 1

On January 28, 1986, the U.S. space shuttle, The Challenger, blew up and the day and my life would never be the same. My total intention was to take the day off from my job and celebrate my birthday by watching the exciting event. The evening prior, I decided to videotape the event and present it to my Uncle John. He loved these historic events. Uncle John had American eagles, American Flags and historical pictures all over his tiny farmhouse and barn. He would love this!!

I awoke that day with great expectations. After settling myself on the couch, in front of the television, the VCR all set and ready to go, and my first cup of coffee in hand, I got that feeling like I always did. I remembered when I was a kid that I always knew prematurely something was going to be wrong. And something wasn't right at all.

I watched intently as they spoke of scraping the ice from the shuttle and said to myself, "Something is not right !" The next sound I heard was a burst of screams and cries from the hundreds of people in the crowd watching as the space shuttle burst in the sky disintegrating only 72 seconds into flight. Red orange flames sparked throughout the skies. I stared at that screen in disbelief. All day it was replayed, and replayed, but my gut feeling said the day was not over. There was something more to come.

Chapter 2

I prepared all afternoon to look extra nice for a special dinner with my boyfriend, Peter, trying to perfect what I felt was not. Peter and I were a thing for a number of years now. Four to be exact. He was a man of my dreams, my friend, my confidant, my lover. I finally was ready and felt good about me; myself. He arrived and kissed my cheek, not saying, or was it, not noticing all the time I put into "looking my best" for him. He hurried me out the door.

"Are you hungry or just in a hurry to get there?" I laughed.

He did not respond. I asked if he watched the space shuttle and he reviewed the event with me with utter technical chatter. Nothing more. Not even a glance my way.

We arrived at our favorite quiet place, The Barstreet Grill, and sat at the back corner table. The waitress was prompt and we ordered our drinks- my usual, Canadian Club and soda ,and Peter, a draft beer. Peter, of course, ordered our meals that we loved to share. The place was a very quiet bar-restaurant where you could have drinks, dinner, and a conversation that you both could hear. But, tonight was different. Oh God! There could have been loud music, and flying crashing bottles of beer and I could still have heard those infamous words.

"Ellen, we've got to talk about us."

I've always been a serene, logical, and willing to listen person, but when I heard those words my body began to shake and my eyes felt like the Carribean. But, I calmly said, "What about us?"

Our drinks had arrived and there was silence as the waitress approached. Then there was more uncomfortable silence as we sipped our drinks; neither of us looked at each other.

Dinner had arrived with no words spoken. The waitress cheerfully smiled and said," Enjoy."

"Let's eat, and then we can talk." Peter announced.

My calmness had started to disintegrate, my appetite disappeared,and my temper rose like a sunset.

“Now!! Let’s talk now.”

Chapter 3

I could hear the words of how there was something wrong, of how the feeling wasn't the same, of how we, we maybe should...

And the only words I could mutter as the tears fell down my face and my throat closed up were, "Why not! The space shuttle blew up on my birthday! Just why not !!"

He looked at me and tried to hug me assuming that would calm me down.

I pulled away and said, "I'm fine. I'm okay." Okay I said to myself, I am under control.

I left the table and searched for the restroom mumbling over and over again " I am in control. I am in control." I looked in the mirror and saw someone I did not know. Was I in control? Was this me ? A beautiful blonde stared at me as she reapplied her lip gloss and smiled. Grinning I looked at her and said, " Have a great night." and walked out.

Returning to the table, “under control” somewhat, I pushed my dinner plate away and ordered another drink .

“You don’t need that right now? “ He stated.

“Oh yes, yes I do. “

How could he say I didn't need that. After 4 years? After a “the end”. I don’t need another drink? Hell I need more!

In the midst of the night, after many empty glasses, we drove back to my apartment. I heard of the mid life crisis, the thrill is gone,ears and I still love you, and tears,and I feel as bad as you, tears, and there is no one else, tears.

And holding and making love, or was it ??

Chapter 4

The morning was silent with my tears. I made him breakfast as usual, or foolishly. He briskly went off to work. I cried, hibernated, and hid from the phone's rings. All day my lab hound, Trevor hung close to me as never before, feeling my pain. The day fell completely to numbness and rejection. He, Peter, returned that evening and we cried together and shared what was said the evening before.The words did not sound any different today than yesterday. My heart drowned in my tears and anger started to flow forth. Words were coming out and I didn't have control of what I was saying or why- until now.

"How could you leave me after all this time?" Why didn't you tell me? Let me go!"

He tried to make me feel as if he was going through as much pain as I. I believed it. And then in a short time he was gone again.

Motionless, I whispered, " Happy Birthday Ellen. Happy Birthday."

Chapter 5

The phone rang at 10:00 am Saturday and I answered with all the confidence I had left.

“Hello”.

Jan was my best friend and work partner. We’ve known each other for only a few years, but felt like a lifetime.

Tears filled my eyes and my throat choked.

“I’m fine”. It came out a little rough.

“Ellen, what’s wrong? I know there is something wrong?”

“I am fine.” and tears fell, and more tears, and more tears.

“Oh, Jan, help me!”

I explained, but how could I explain when I couldn’t even understand myself, or was it that I didn’t want to accept even the thought of it. Maybe I could just put the birthday present back in the box and try to return it without the receipt. Maybe they could exchange it?

It didn't work. Jan could not even say the right words this time to help me right now. She offered to come over, but I declined. Jan said she would be there if I wanted to talk. I wanted to be alone and think this out for myself. She understood. And as the day wore on I realized that my birthday present was a goodbye. Nothing boxed, no ribbon, just a simple rip of emotion. Sleep was my only resort to not believing the horror.

So, I slept and slept.

The alarm didn't ring that Sunday, but something rang in my mind at 6 am. I looked around, but nothing was the same. The lamp on the dresser, the pictures on the walls were all clouded. I unconsciously poured two cups of coffee and drank both myself. I took a shower, dressed and ran out of the house as if something was going to be there. But it wasn't. Nothing was there that I could see anyway. So I went wearily inside.

I didn't have to accept anything that happened, so I dialed the phone and called him as usual. He wouldn't talk. Only asked if I was alright, how was my sanity, how were my tears, have I talked to anyone at all yet. And then as if he said "I've done enough consoling" - I heard a dial tone….

Chapter 6

There is always a time in your life when someone, "we call a friend", comes out of the woodwork to say "I understand how you feel." In my case, I called Jan, my psychiatrist (not really, but a good listener). She listened, and guided and said "I think I understand". Things as they went got ugly. I ran the course. I didn't eat, didn't sleep, and drank like a fish, but it didn't even touch my emotional state. Peter tried harder and harder to leave without any attachments. No visits. No calls. I'll never forget those ugly words he spoke.

"You're not pretty, you have no ambition, no energy, and you're no fun."

So vulnerable, I believed the words. I believed the lies. There still was "no one else in his life." he repeated.

His sister, Bea and her husband tried often to help me, but couldn't (or wouldn't) give me answers. I called Bea and pleaded with her, "Bea, what did I do? What happened?"

Finally, she broke down. She spoke of this other woman and how everyone knew.

Except me!!

She reiterated all the ugly words he said to me and she made me promise to never let him know she told me. I kept my promise to this day.

We hung up crying. I hung up crying in anger.

I made a promise to Jan that I would not call him again. I promised and I lied. I had to call him. I did. As I dialed I shook. I waited what seemed to be forever, hanging onto every tone of the rings. He answered in someone else's voice, someone else's attitude.

"Don't call again." He hung up.

Chapter 7

I called back. Another voice answered. Oh God! It was a female voice that told me she wished I wouldn't call anymore. It was as if hell had fired me up and set me off, just like the space shuttle.

He got on the phone.

"Look, I told you it was over."

Over, no! He spoke of mid life crisis, of taking time off from each other, maybe then things would get better, of no one else in his life.

Over NOOO!!!

Those words were not part of my vocabulary. So I told him. Plainly, rudely, viciously. The words flowed out of my mouth like a gushing oil well. My final terms were 5:30, my house, the next day.

I called my psych. The phone rang, and I heard Jan's voice, and screamed, "Jan, take me to the hospital! I got to go, I'm out of control. I am going fucking crazy!"

"Ellen, calm down. Talk to me. You are okay."

I told her of my findings and never in my life have I felt such a feeling. My body rose from the bed and floated to God knows where. I couldn't stabilize anything about myself. Crying, I could not breath, but tried to talk. Jan listened and listened. She succeeded in calming me. My body settled back to bed, but that's where it laid awake all night.

Jan picked me up for work the next day. I don't know how I got dressed, but I did look extra good (just in case). Plan 2 had to come into effect now.

Plan 2 : He doesn't show .You find him.

Chapter 8

The next day, the first day of a different life . Anticipating all day that evening's meeting, I didn't plan on him showing. Except for Jan, I kept my secret. I didn't want the publicity and the "I'm sorries" that usually go alone with a break up. My psych and I did agree on one thing. I had to briefly tell my boss so she would understand why I was bouncing off of walls, and glaring at things that weren't there, and babbling about nothing at all.

Chapter 9

I did. I sat in her office chair like I was sentenced to death. Palms sweating, eyes tearing, voice shaking and babbled about something or everything..

"I'm sorry, Kate. I shouldn't be out of control. I'm a supervisor and should be able to handle this. I can handle this."

"Ellen. It's okay. Just stay strong and if you need me I am here. Okay?"

I must have said thank you ten million times. She understood and smiled gently.

It was finally 5:00 o'clock and I had no sleep, but I still had the energy like the 20 mule team. As Jan and I drove home, I rambled on about how I didn't think he was going to show.

"Call me if that happens. I'll drive you anywhere you want to go. I promise". Jan exclaimed.

"Okay!" I slammed the car door and walked cautiously to my apartment door and went in. I turned on the stereo softly and poured myself a glass of chardonnay. I must have touched up my makeup and hair ten times and then.

I was startled by the doorbell's ring. Oh God, it rang ! I went to the door looking confident, smiling, but cautious. My insides churning with anxiety. It was Peter. He walked in hesitantly with shame on his face. A total blank expression as he slithered to the chair.

"I really did it all wrong. I'm sorry." he said.

I felt something leave my body, like some kind of force passing and being replaced by nothing. Just an empty space. There was silence for a minute or two, or was it an hour.

"What do you want me to say? I don't know what to say. Why don't you just tell me the truth?"

"I just wasn't happy anymore," he said sheepishly.

"And you are happy now? I made you that incredibly miserable?" I said calmly.

"No. It just wasn't working for a couple of years now." Peter stated.

My temper rose.

“A couple of years and now you decide to tell me?”

Chapter 10

"I didn't know how, and I guess I didn't do it very well." he hesitated. " I hope we can be friends?"

"No, you didn't." Ellen looked puzzled and confused. "Friends?"

What the hell was this shit?

"You're happier now, right Peter?"

"Yes, Ellen, I am."

In the back of my mind was "right, yeah, you're happier. You have someone to be there for you. I don't. But I couldn't let him know I knew. My face got warm, I guess the old blood pressure rose a bit after that thought.

Silence again.

Then it slid out of my mouth. "You know this is a lot easier for you than me ?"

"No. It isn't".

He tried to sound sympathetic knowing all along that she was there for him.

I almost rose to hit him at that point, but realized that it wouldn't make a difference. He really didn't care. But friends? Oh God, come on!

"It's going to be a long time before I can trust you. And friends? God I'll try but …."

"I think I better go."

"I think so too." My mind kept going, but what about .. and I still tried to cling on and I did, for a while. But….

And then Peter was gone.

Chapter 11

Rrring !!!

I answered the phone and heard laughter. Female laughter.

"Why don't you just stay out of our lives. He doesn't want you anymore. Why can't you just let him go." she screeched like nails on a chalkboard.

Click.

I slid to the floor and cried.

I did receive calls from Peter's sister and husband, and his Mom, but what could they do to help me? They tried to make me laugh, but to no avail. Bea, Peter's sister, relayed that a mutual friend was interested in maybe going out sometime in hopes to make me feel better. I debated, then flatly refused saying,

"It's too soon. It's all too strange. I don't know."

I brought it up to Jan afterwards and she agreed that a mutual friend was not a good choice. I dialed my family time and time again to talk, but hung up before they answered. Still not ready for all of that explanation. I tried to reach my close cousin, Tom, (he was somewhat of a brother to me), but each time there was no answer and I hung up leaving no message. I couldn't talk or even understand it all yet.

Chapter12

Saturday again with nothing planned. I finally convinced myself that I needed to get out. I needed to talk. I reached for the phone and dialed hoping to get Tom.

"Hello." the deep voice answered.

"Oh, thank God you answered. Hi. What's up?" my voice shook.

"Not much. Yourself?"

"Oh well nothing really. Well I mean …."

"Is there something up, something wrong?" Tom could always tell when I wasn't myself. "You need to talk?"

"Yeah." my voice slumped. There was a pause in the conversation.

"I'll tell you what. I don't have plans tonight. Let's go out and have a drink."

"Great!" I answered with a smile of relief.

"See you around eight. Is that okay Ellen?"

"Yes, yes. Good."

As soon as we hung up, the phone rang. That angry voice echoed, " Stay out of our lives bitch!!"

I slammed the receiver down and closed my eyes, shaking. My mind over and over said "Let it go.Let it go", and finally my body calmed. Glancing at the clock I hurried to get ready for the night. I caught myself staring in the mirror smiling.

"Looking good Ellen." I laughed and nodded to my reflection.

Tom arrived promptly at eight. We talked and talked, and he listened to the Peter story with raised eyebrows.

"I really need a drink , Tom".

"Where do you want to go? "

"Well..."

"Well, where?"

Chapter 13

“I want to go back to the place of those infamous words of “ We’ve got to talk”. I want to show those people that yes I did survive and I’m alright. As a matter of fact I’m great.”

“Your choice!”

Tom ushered me out to the car and followed my directions to The Barstreet Grill.

Everyone there knew us. Peter and Ellen. But, they did not know Tom. So I had a date! Right?

Before we walked in, I stopped, and took a deep breath at the door.

“Are you okay?” Tom asked.

I flashed a great big smile and said, “I’m fine. As a matter of fact, I’m great. I just have to do this, you know?”

“Let’s do this!” Tom laughed.

As we walked in, Tom as always, the utmost gentleman, opened the door and gave me my choice of seating. Familiar faces turned and gazed. My eyes focused on Tom as I led the way to what was "our" favorite table. Ordering our drinks, Tom, his bourbon on the rocks and my C.C. and soda, the waitress smiled and stared momentarily. I was unsure if she was giving me a sign of approval or just a sign of pleasantry. Tom and I talked and talked about our jobs and people and fun vacations,but not Peter. My mind felt clear and alive again.

And my smile did not disappear from the time we got there until the time we left, and then again the whole night long. As we left, I felt eyes upon us, but kept my focus. My smile did not dissipate.

Chapter 14

Tom took me to several of his hang outs. He tried his damndest to get me loaded so I would loosen up. It was working.

"Oh, by the way, I told Jim we were going out. Do you remember Jim?" Tom asked.

Yes, I remember back in 1978, before I met Peter, he took me to lunch. Nothing ever materialized. Not sure what happened, but I do remember lunch was nice.

"He will probably meet us here."

I smiled. "Fine, no problem."

I thought nothing of it. Tom's friend did show up at the second bar we went to. He remembered me, but not quite the way I looked now, but he remembered. He looked the same. The typical Italian boy look that could have stepped out of the GQ magazine. He was aloof and a bit arrogant and just leaned against the bar adding to the conversation as he looked around. He didn't even notice me until I became arrogant and sarcastic with my quick comebacks.

Tom proceeded to talk and joke, and kept ordering drinks. They were both shelling peanuts from the bar and throwing the shells on the floor while I was placing them in a tidy pile atop the bar.

Tom grabbed my arm and laughed, “Here, be assertive. Just throw them on the floor. That’s what they expect us to do with the shells.”

I looked at Jim with all his arrogance. He gazed off into space expecting us to catch his part of the conversation from the air.

“You know Tom. I can’t just throw these on the floor. It just does nothing for me. Now I can do this.”

I grabbed a peanut and flung it across the room nearly missing Jim’s face, bouncing it against the side of the wall.

Chapter 15

“Now that did something for me.“ I smirked.

Jim turned leaning on the bar and looked at me, now smiling and laughing.

“You know, I’ve been listening to you all night and you are crazy, but you are really one together lady.”

I laughed hysterically at that comment.
“Me.Together?” I thought. Our eyes met for the first time that night and smiled.

“Hey, let’s get something to eat before we close this place.” Tom announced.

As we walked out deciding on where to grab a late night snack, Tom turned to me.

“You need to see Jim’s new Porsche?”

I glared at the beautiful, black, shiny new sports car.

“Hey, can I ride in the new car?” I asked without a thought. Tom smiled.

Jim escorted me to the car and I settled in.

“You like?” he inquired, smiling.

"Yeah, I approve." I smiled back.

We met Tom at the old diner, The Midnight Seven..Tom and Jim ordered breakfast, and I, coffee.

"Not hungry?" Tom asked. "

"I'm good. Thanks."

We joked about the evening and chattered about late night antics.

"I'll ride Ellen home if ok?" Jim looked up at Tom taking his last bite.

I looked at Tom. He approved and smiled.

As Jim drove, my eyes observed his words as we talked and laughed a lot.

After the night's end, Jim and I decided we did want to see each other again. So, I left my number on the dashboard without much thought.

We arrived at my apartment, I smiled at his attempt at a good night kiss. I was not ready.

“Good night or Good morning.” I whispered as I got out of the car. He watched as I opened the door and waved. It was 4 am when I arrived home. I slept a few hours and awoke as usual, confused and alone.

Chapter 16

I'm not pretty, have no ambition, no energy and I'm no fun. Who the hell is that? NOT ME!

I started looking in the mirror practically every twenty minutes. Played with my hair, my makeup and became more aware of who I was, rather than who I was supposed to be for him. Jan and I talked practically everyday and reviewed our day's ventures. Mainly, Jan checking up on me. I would look at myself in the mirror as we talked. I felt more and more of me come back to me. Laughter became easier. As a matter of fact, everything was becoming more fun. I went shopping for Me. My "psych", Jan, drug me out to buy new clothes and shoes. It felt good to spend time and money on myself. I worked every chance I got and loved talking to anyone about practically anything.

Weekends came quickly. I started getting more and more restless. I decided that this particular Friday I would take someone up on his offer. So the new me, the outgoing fun me, decided to call him up. Except? I didn't have a number. So, do I dare call Peter's sister?

“Hey, Bea! I kind of decided to take Rob up on his offer. Do you think he’d mind if I called him?”

“No, go for it!

I heard Bea rustling pages. Here’s his number.“ she said enthusiastically. “Have fun !”

I did not hesitate.

Rring!! Rring!

“Hi, Hey! This is Ellen.”

“Hi!” a surprised voice responded.

“Hey,I was wondering, would you like to go out and have a drink with me tonight if you're not busy.”

Chapter 17

Rob said he was sitting for a friend's dog and it just so happened to be down the street from me. Hmm!

"Great, I'll pick you up at nine. Good?"

I did. He did. And we did.

We went to a small bar,The Shadyside Bar, and talked, and talked, and laughed and compared adventures. For the first time in years I found someone that actually listened to me, heard me, accepted me, and my ideas and dreams. After a few drinks, we decided to leave, but he didn't want to end the night. Nor did I. He stared at me as we got into the car. He looked at me, and then said the most peculiar thing.

"Can I kiss you?" he asked sweetly.

Our lips and smiles met.

"Is this just a one night thing?" he questioned.

"I don't think so".

We kissed at stop signs, red lights and laughed when we saw both of us with one eye on the light. It was the last light before my apartment. He stopped at a yellow light and of course it turned red. Everything seemed to be right. He looked at me long and smiled and shook his head.

"I can't believe you. You make me feel like I am in high school. You've got so much life, energy, and so fun to be with."

I just smiled. He couldn't know what those words meant to me.

"What would you like to do?"

"Let's take the dogs to the park!".

He glanced at his watch. "It's two in the morning."

Smiles. Giggling I said, " And you know an hour ago it was one."

"Let's go! We'll pick up Bo first. Alright?"

Confidently, I walked into his friend's house, his ex girlfriend's house. He said he was dog sitting for her while she was out of town. He explained to me of how they remained friends. She always despised me for some reason. I could never understand it.

Chapter 18

We were welcomed by Bo at the door and prepared him for his adventure. Strolling to my apartment we kissed under the street lights, just like in the movies I thought. The night was warm and quiet. He tied Bo outside of my apartment door and we retrieved my dog, Trevor. Dogs on leashes we strolled to the park hand and hand. But somehow the dogs had their own ideas crossing back and forth, and back and forth. Entering the park, he let Bo go his way. A little leary, but after I was swept off my feet, we laid beneath the blossomed tree,and I let go of Trevor. It was all like something in a dream..

That night we parted in hopes to see each other again the next evening. We did. He called practically every other day there after.

Chapter 19

The park was 2 minutes from my apartment so I frequently caught the little league baseball games, and any chance I could to catch the rays. I noticed a lot more around me now. I took Trevor there every evening after work and on weekends. Later this Sunday afternoon, I decided Trevor and I were due for a game and walk. I loved the kids, the people, the sun, everything.

We walked to the park and sat on the grassy hillside watching the game. A man approached us and started talking to Trevor. I looked at him and laughed.

“Hi ! Do you mind if I join you?” he said to Trevor.

“No, I think he is fine with it.” I smiled.

He sat down on the hillside beside us. He was an athletic, muscular man with broad shoulders and a wide smile to match. We chatted about the little league game and pets. For some odd reason I felt as if I knew him.

“By the way I’m John. John Schmitt.” he announced.

"Ellen." I grinned

"Want to take a walk?" he asked, looking at Trevor anxious to roam. Oddly I didn't hesitate, not at all.

We went down the trail and he looked at me. "It's kind of strange you would take a walk with me down here."

I stopped and faced him.

"Do I know you from somewhere?" I asked inquisitively. "I could swear I met you before. And no, not strange that I would take a walk." I quirked back. "Did you know my dog bites odd people that ask strange questions!!!"

I laughed and so did he.

He had strange questions and I had quick comebacks. What a pair. He was between a decision of two jobs and asked me for my opinion. Both jobs in sales. I saw his personality in both. I chattered away thinking " why not, he asked."

From one end of the park to the other we talked. By the time we got back to our starting point it was like we were old friends, until he asked if he could walk me home. My defenses went up like a fourth of July flag and hung heavy. But I agreed. This man, I didn't even know, to boot an ex football player as I learned, looked larger and larger at my home base. I was a tad bit frightened, but I went into the house and wrote my number down. I did want to see him again. And maybe again. I handed him the paper and he said "I'll call you." I started to laugh, somehow envisioning so many years of "the I'll call yous" that never produced. He laughed too and said,

"There is just something about you. You're fun!" I smiled and shook my head walking towards the door.

"I really have to get my work done. See ya."

Back in my apartment, I started doing my job work that I had planned on doing all weekend, but somehow it always got put on the back burner. It was time to face facts. This is Sunday night, get to it.

Thirty minutes later the phone rang and I answered.

"Hi, just wondered if you were finished and maybe we could do something tonight."

It was John.

"You just wanted to see if I really gave you the right number, huh?"

"Okay, I just thought I'd ask." he laughed. "I'll try again."

We hung up. I smiled.

Jan called and we had a session of what are days entailed over the phone. She wasn't surprised at anything that happened to me anymore, as long as I was careful.

Every night of the week I tried to keep myself busy with walks with Trevor at the park or by myself. Going here and there and everywhere. And yes, John and I did go out. Only for a couple of drinks during the week to start. We enjoyed each other's company and I felt comfortable enough with him to explain my situation. "THE BIG BREAKUP!" He listened and listened. And sometimes we would just look at each other and laugh. Nothing said, nothing done, just burst out with laughter. John and I became good friends for now.

Chapter 20

Spring was finally here. The rain, the leaves,the flowers and bright skies made me feel like I was growing within it. Even at work, people were asking "What happened to you. You look fantastic. What's your secret, what's going on in your life." Still,I kept my secret and smiled and didn't stop smiling or making people laugh.

I called Jan and started with utter chit chat. Looking out the window, my voice escalated.

"Jan, he's always there!"

"Who?"

"This guy in his car outside my window!"

"What? You mean that guy you told me about a couple weeks ago. Why didn't you tell me?"

"Oh, you know, it's stupid. He's there when I leave for work in the morning and when I come home from work. He's probably just got a fetish for reading in his car." I laughed.

"Ellen, you need to start keeping a log. You should notify the police, just in case. "

"Oh ok, if it makes you happy." I smirked.

"Ellen." Jan's voice dropped with concern.

I didn't call the police, but started noting dates and times, and slid it in my top dresser drawer thinking this is stupid, but…

White Toyota

7:05 am April 10

5:30 pm April 13

7:10 am April 15

Chapter 21

My job was fantastic. I could hardly wait to go back after a weekend and to be around all the people. I did fear being alone, and being alone with the phone. I still couldn't talk about anything to my family and when I did talk to them I was very evasive. Everything was fine. Nothing wrong. I was well aware that they knew better.

Finally, I called my sister, Julie. I made her promise she wouldn't say a word to our parents and I cried and cried on the phone. Her husband, Dave wanted to kill Peter for hurting me. I pleaded with Julie to not let him go or say anything to Peter. She promised. Julie and Dave spent the day with me in an attempt to try to help me relax and to make me realize that it was going to be okay.

I kept thinking," No, it is not going to be okay". I smiled anyway for the way they cared. I was appreciative of what they were trying to do, but I needed to get back home to my life. Trevor awaited my return with excitement, prancing and wagging his tail with glee.

I saw my friend outside more and more often now. His car was parked outside my apartment and now he appeared at the park. I decided that it was time to contact the police. They told me to start keeping a log with dates, times, make of car, description, and they would have a car police the area.

“Yes, my friend already told me to do that. I am doing it now.” I announced.

“What, who’s your friend, a cop?”

“No! My, my.. I almost said psych,but didn’t.

“Good. Keep us notified. If this continues the next couple days we’ll have someone out again.“

“Okay. Thank you.”

Preparing for the next day, I said to myself, “God,I’ve got to wear something I feel good in. Sometimes feeling good makes all the bad disappear. I pulled out the navy skirt with white chiffon blouse grinning. Yeah, here it was. Perfect! I glanced out the window. He was there again.

Dark, curly hair, grubby beard, mustache, looks kind of stalky. I noted it all and left it on my dresser ignoring what was behind the now pulled curtains. I slept soundly believing there was nothing there.

When Jan picked me up the next day, I felt great. The birds were chirping away and I noticed dew drops on the tree. I said "Good Morning" to everyone these days and really meant it. Life was exciting now, but I still thought of him. Peter. It still wasn't easy. My boss constantly gave me new duties to do. Interviewing new employees was next. I was petrified, but after the first, I enjoyed it so much. Each new person I met was a new person not in our life, but my life. One particular male employee, and I mean "Male", started to get very friendly. Every girl in the whole medical staff "wanted him." My opinion was that he was okay. He knows that he is good looking, probably married or something. The man was built, you could see every muscle, and that smile he flashed (you know, like one of those commercials). Oh, come on !!

I got used to racing down the long hallway to do copying, get supplies, do my interviews which passed the Physical therapy department where he worked. I never paid much attention except to say Good Morning to Bob, the department manager. Jan grabbed me on the way back to hand me a bunch of paperwork and repeated "this needs updated and this updated." I smiled and shook my head and headed on down the hallway back to the office.

"Hey Jan, thanks." I said sarcastically laughing. As I walked past the therapy department and started rounding the corner, a head popped out of the door.

"Hey, thanks."

I turned around and looked at this gorgeous man, "the every girl wanted him guy", and glanced at him inquisitively.

"For what?" my eyes squinted.

"Just for walking by." he said in a whispery voice.

"No problem, you're welcome." I looked at him, smiled, shaking my head in confusion, and returned to my office to find notes and more messages. One note stated - "I need this ASAP. Thanks Kate."

Okay. Write it, type it, copy it now. I rushed the order through and proceeded back to the copier to find that head still popping out of the door.

"Hey, how is your day going?"

"Just fine and yours? "

"It's Friday, big weekend planned? "

"I'm just trying to make it through today. What's your problem? "

"Are you doing anything Sunday? I thought maybe I could take you out to Dunkin Donuts for breakfast?"

I looked at him like he was nuts and said "Dunkin Donuts, sure?" and laughed.

"Well, can I call you?"

I hesitated, but then started writing my number down,shaking my head mumbling "Dunkin Donuts". I ripped the paper off and stopped.

"I don't usually give my number out , but this is too bizarre to pass up".

"Talk to you later." he said smiling and closing the door.

I was intrigued and puzzled. I kept it a secret and smiled to myself all afternoon.

Jan stopped me in the hall with her work bags.

"Yeah, Jan! It's Friday !" It was a long and hectic week. The sun shone bright in the car and we wound down the windows.The warm breeze felt amazing on the way home. Arriving at my apartment, I opened the car door, and Jan gave me a great weekend smile. She knew I had a Friday and Saturday date planned.

"Yeah, I know I can't believe it either. Friday, Saturday and a possible date for breakfast Sunday. Sunday, I am not quite sure about it yet."

I shut the door before Jan could even question me. I didn't want to tell her because somehow, well, I thought maybe she would sway my answer to that date. I didn’t think he’d call anyway.

Chapter 22

I got ready to meet John for our end of the week, "comparative notes of the week date." I noticed that man outside once again in his car, noted it, and placed it in the top dresser drawer without much thought. It seemed to be just another task to do anymore. I hurried to get ready knowing John would be there soon. He greeted me at the door with a grin and hug. I felt his eyes follow me as I rushed to grab my purse across the room. We went out for a few drinks at his favorite bar and talked, and talked, and laughed a lot. John and I always had a good time together, but when it came to a good night, it always made me nervous. I don't know why. Something just held me back and I hated my ex for doing this to me. It was just this shield that slammed in front of me any time closeness was involved. John was very much a gentleman about it . He always seemed to understand, but I knew in the back of my mind that one day he wouldn't and I would lose him. That's when my anger would get out of hand because I hated Peter for making me feel this way. It was as if he had some kind of power force and he would wait for those moments and hex me with this spell. The night ended and John kissed my cheek, smiled as we said our goodnights.

Saturday morning I awoke early as usual. I still had a bad habit of pouring two cups of coffee. This time I emptied one down the kitchen sink. Kind of felt good. It was a gorgeous day. Nothing planned, but sometimes that was fun. Usually, I'd go work out, but oh how I started to hate taking that bus. My Dad was still looking for a car for me, but nothing came about yet, at least that I could afford anyway. So, I made the best out of bussing it. The morning went fast and the day faster. When the sun started setting I called to see what Jan was doing.

"Hi, How was last night?"

"Oh fine. You know I always enjoy being with John."

'What are you doing tonight?"

"Zennin is taking me out? "

“Great! “

“Jan, this guy is still out here. And yes,I know. I am keeping track of everything, but he’s starting to get on my nerves. I just feel like going up to him and saying, “What’s your problem?”

“No, don’t do that !” she said alarmingly.

“I have a call beeping in Jan. Can you hold on a sec?”

“Hello!”

“Hi sexy, how are you? This is Roman.” his whispery voice sang.

My mouth dropped open wide. I said to myself, ”Come on Ellen. Come up with something witty.”

“Hey, you know this isn’t Sunday yet. Is it ? Did I miss something?“

“Busy?”

“No. I was just deciding what I wanted to do tonight?”

“Well, if you are free,how would you like some company? “

“I’m up for suggestions.” I shut my eyes thinking that was the wrong thing to say.

“Well, I could come over and bring some bubbly or we could go somewhere”

The automatic shield came up! Come over.Bubbly. Oh no, not safe.

“Do you want to go out for a drink, dance, whatever?” he suggested.

“That sounds nice.”

“9:30?“ Ok. See you then.”

“Yes,ok.” Click.

“Jan, are you still there? I panicked.” Jan, I don’t know what I am getting into?”

“Does this have to do with … What did you mean by “breakfast Sunday?”

"That was Roman. He asked me out. I don't understand what he wants from me. I mean you know he is gorgeous! Me?"

" Ellen." Jan said. "Don't worry about it. He must be interested. You're pretty, realize it. Forget about what Peter said. Just be careful."

"What do I wear, something safe huh?" I laughed.

"Maybe a jumpsuit. That's safe as long as we don't play strip poker." We both laughed.

"Jan, I am a nervous wreck. I haven't had an actual first date in well, a long time."

"Just go out, calm down, have fun and be careful. Call me if you need me."

"I'll let you know where we are going?"

"Good."

I changed clothes ten times and ended up with the first thing I had on as usual. Pale pink jumpsuit and pink leather heels. Rummaging for my earrings I looked in the mirror. I paused and thought to myself, “You look good. Yes, you do. Alright, we’re ready! “

The doorbell rang and I froze, my heart pounding a bit.

Proceeding to the door, I opened it and there he was; gorgeous, looking good. I directed him into my apartment. He looked at me and smiled. Trevor greeted him with a wagging tail. That to me was a good sign.

“Hey there,buddy.” he said, reaching down to pet Trevor. As he arose his eyes he grinned.

“How did you know I liked jumpsuits?”

“I didn’t, but thanks. “

“You better grab a coat or something. Supposed to get cold later.” he stated. Oh no, I hadn’t thought of that. Which one,I panicked. I think I made him nervous too. I decided on the short fur and pulled my purse onto my shoulder. He escorted me out holding each door while I locked up.

As we walked outside, he directed me to a white VET. My heart pounded, but I remained calm. “Gorgeous car!” I thought to myself. He opened the door and I settled in as much as I could, seeing that my nerves were just a little on the “first date” side. We chatted inquiring about each other in bits and pieces and arrived at Station Square, parked and headed for the night spot. We both got carded at the door. He passed. I handed my driver’s license to the doorman. He looked at me.

“Sorry mame.”

I looked back at him and smiled. “ Please don’t call me mame.” He smiled and laughed. Roman grabbed my arm gently and laughed.

“That’s quite a compliment, don’t be embarrassed.”

We checked our coats and I signed for my fur. He laughed whispering, “ A fur, classy”.

Heading for the bar he grasped my hand gently and said, “ I don’t want to lose you in the crowd.”

We made it there safely together.

“What can I get you?” he asked grinning.

“C.C and soda please.” I smiled back. He ordered a gin and tonic. We sipped our drinks and leaned against the bar watching the dance crowd. He was full of questions. His questioning made me feel as if he was truly interested in my life, in me. I started to feel very much at ease.

“Can I ask you something Roman?”

He nodded.

“Why me, I mean, I thought you had a girlfriend, wife or something. I mean I worked there awhile and…”

He stopped me. “Because you’re different and I wanted to get to know you. Okay? And no I’m not married or have a girlfriend!” He laughed. “I enjoy people and life and there is no one tying me down now.”

Subject dropped. It was okay. More than ok. And I wanted to tell Jan.

We watched people, and laughed, and smiled a lot. All of a sudden he leaned over and kissed my cheek. I didn't even turn to look at him. Just smiled.

"Do you mind?" he asked as our eyes met.

"Not at all. Thank you. That was very nice."

We tried to dance, but the dance floor was so crowded it was next to impossible.

"Do you want to go?" he asked.

"Fine. I think I'm getting claustrophobic!"

As we tried to make our way out, he turned and knocked over a bottle of beer on the table beside us. He apologized to the girl so sweetly . Something I've rarely seen in a bar. She accepted.

"I am really embarrassed." he sincerely said to me.

"Hey, it was your turn." I laughed. "I hope I don't have to see the doorman again."

He grasped my hand tightly now, retrieved our coats, and put his arm around me gently.

It was chilly outside, but he kept me warm until we reached the car.

"Is it alright if we go back to your place?" he asked sweetly.

"Yes." I nodded.

He reached over to me pulling me towards him, held my hand and gave me a warm , gentle kiss. I looked at him. "Home please Roman."

He smiled sweetly.

That moment I knew in my heart that for four years I was missing something. This is where I belonged. This is what was meant for me. This is what I truly deserved. To be treated like royalty. This was only a dream for maybe one evening, but I was going to live and enjoy it. I was actually smiling from my heart. And I loved it, I lived the dream.

We entered my apartment. His kiss was passionate.

"You know, if we were playing strip poker, you would lose." he smiled.

I was stunned by the familiar humor.

If that was losing, I thought to myself, what would winning be like.

Suddenly his hands and tongue and thighs were exactly where I had been dying for them to be. I accepted each caress without any second thought, but somehow I saw Peter in my mind.

"Hey, do I still have a date for Dunkin Donuts?" I smirked.

We laughed holding each other ever so tight, sweat from his body pouring on me. Still kissing me gently and holding my hand, he got ready to leave that early am.

"You know, I never imagined.." he stopped in mid sentence.

"What, what?"

"You're so much fun to be with "

I smiled and smiled as he walked out the door.

Chapter 23

Jan called me later on that morning. "Well how did it go? I didn't get a call from you?" she joked.

"Just, just fine. I really enjoyed myself. I had a fantastic time. I don't know what I was worried about. I just really enjoyed being me."

"I don't know?" she said with a question in her voice. She always had a way of saying that. You knew she wanted to add more, she was thinking more, but just let it fade. It always made me feel like she was saying, "I know something, but you figure it out for yourself because then it means much more to you. Grow with it, take that knowledge and grow and learn. I always wondered whether this woman was Superman's mother or something.

"So what's up today?"

"What are Sundays for, Jan? "

Laundry early, shower, dress, coffee and out the door. Catch some rays, relax, have some fun, meet people, go CRAZY! Don't think.

What else is on the list. Oh yeah, chart your followers' car outside your apartment and following you to the park and…. I was getting angry with it now. JUST STOP !! I kept thinking “leave me alone. Let me live my life.” Thoughts poured through my mind like a sieve. Why and who is doing this to me. I kept thinking of Peter and reasons. Maybe he wants to know if, and who I am dating, if I am happy. Was he jealous? Did he still care? Was he having someone watch me ? The day flew by and my thoughts remained unanswered . The only answer I had was that I was getting used to having fun.

Preparing for the next day and a big meeting, I searched for something to wear,something nice, something that said “me.” Yep, here it was. Glancing out the window as I held the green sleeveless linen dress, I saw that white car again. I drew the blinds on him, on everything. The phone rang and my mind stopped and laughed. Who cares!! You are actually happy. No car. No Peter. I answered the phone. It was Roman. I felt a calmness.

“Hi sexy. How are you? We talked, we joked, we laughed. See you tomorrow. Say hello to me in the hallway. Okay?”

“Yeah.Okay?. See ya.”

My mind and my heart fell asleep soundly that night.

Chapter 24

Jan picked me up the next morning as usual. We said our "Good mornings" to Ray, the security guard and quickly arrived at our working posts. I directed my first group of employees to attend the 8:00 am meeting with our President and VP waiting to begin. They returned with a few comments and I in turn followed the rest to the second attendance. Comparative notes, instructions and support that the company is stable and basically "a let's talk" meeting. Questions were limited from employees and the meeting ended. Our VP, J.R.interrupted with a "Before you leave, I'd like to speak on behalf of our company in regards to one of your fellow employees. It was our usual Outstanding Employee Award presentation. My mind somewhat drifted. And then, I heard my name announced! Tears welled up in my eyes and I was asked to rise to accept my recognition. ME! I couldn't believe it. ME! Outstanding recognition! I was on cloud nine. Jan and my boss beamed. Shaking with excitement, I accepted the recognition, a $100 check, and dinner award with ten million thank yous. I glowed with a feeling of success, of approval, of acceptance. As I walked from the meeting, my legs felt a little like Gumby. I accepted congratulations from fellow employees. Tears still filtered my eyes. Bob and Roman looked at me and tried to persuade me to go to breakfast with them. Still stunned and not knowing what just happened I didn't even answer. I turned around quickly and then blurted out,

"I can't talk. I just won an award. I'm so excited." and I kept walking away. They both just smiled watching me walk down the hallway.

Later that afternoon, Roman sat in the waiting room near my office waiting for me to walk by, waiting to speak to me.

"Hey, what's up?"

"I'm so excited. I just won an award. I'm really excited."

"I know. That's no surprise. This calls for a celebration. See you tonight. Elevenish?

"Oh that sounds really good."

I stood there amazed. He actually was happy for me, almost as excited as me. Peter never would have reacted that way. Oh, he would have said, "Oh that's nice." and would have let it pass.   This was my day, my time, and it could not have come at a better time. People said I glowed.

Roman came through that night with the bubbly, and laughter, and sweet words, and the love. And I glowed some more.

Chapter 25

Days and evenings went quickly, but joyfully. Before I knew, it was time for the weekend and time for fun. Roman usually joined me on Fridays. Passionate, hot evenings. This particular night, I got a call from my Dad.

"Come look at this car. It looks good to me." He described the tawny brown, Chevette, leather interior and some mechanic talk that I didn't really understand, but I listened intently.

"Tomorrow good? I'll meet you."

"Sounds great!"

I called Jan. "Hey, I got a car to look at. Could you…" Before I got the words out she said, "Of course, yes. Give me details."

Excited, we made tomorrow's plans. We met Dad at the dealer and checked out the little Chevette.

"Great mileage - 1600 miles and in good shape. Runs great." he said.

"Go for it ! " Jan shouted.

I did. I bought it with no second thoughts. I could pick it up next week.

Dad drove me back to my apartment and was pleased by my purchase. When we arrived, he walked in and looked around.

"Do you need help with anything?"

"Well, if you are asking, can you help with the air conditioner?"

"Sure. Well how did you put this in the window before?"

"Dad, don't ask, you know who did it for me. Peter."

He worked around any questions and fitted every part together and turned it on. I felt the cool air immediately filling the room.
"There you go. All finished. Anything else?"

"Yeah. I need a hug real bad. He hugged me as to never let go.

"I love you Daddy."

“Same here. Call us. If you need something, don’t be so stubborn.“

My dad never came out and said anything about Peter. I just knew what he meant. Anything that hurt me, hurt him.

“Thanks for everything !” I shouted as he went out the door.

“Lock the door. Be careful. See you this week.” he yelled back.

I saw that man in the car outside and followed my Dad’s instructions. Somehow I felt as if he knew the whole story even though life had not written it yet. Trevor ran from door to window barking up a storm. It startled me at first at how fierce he sounded. He, too, knew something was the matter,but my thoughts switched quickly to the excitement of my new car.

Chapter 26

Roman came to visit practically every night now. It was exciting every time we spent time together. I couldn't wait to tell him about my car because he was always so enthusiastic about anything that made me happy. That's why every moment we spent together became so precious to me. I always knew the romance wouldn't last, but the friendship we had between each other would never end no matter where we were or who we were with. As long as we were happy that was all that counted.

"Roman. You're never going to believe what I did today!"

"What? " he inquisitively asked.

"I bought a car. Now don't laugh? It's a "78 "Chevette with 1,600 miles."

"You mean 16,000 ?" he questioned.

"No I don't!"

Where did you find it, that's great." He grabbed me and hugged me tighter and tighter and didn't let go the entire night.

The evening with Roman went by fast and the morning came quickly, but excitement always filled my days. Sometimes I hated to sleep because I thought I would miss something.

The next morning at work I saw Kate in her office.

“Did you spend all of your money yet?”

“Yeah, I sure did. I bought a car.”

“Really! That’s great ! Now nothing is going to stop you!!“ She laughed.

Work always went by quickly. I enjoyed every minute of being around people. All day, I had Secretary’s Day on my mind. I forgot, I had to get my secretaries something for tomorrow. I’d have to run out after work. Jan had to work late, so I took the bus home. I ran to the store quickly, bought flowers ,cards and ran back to my apartment. Rounding the corner I saw my friend in the car and anger started to well up inside me. I looked at him as I walked past, he glanced up from his paper. Locking my apartment door, I went to the phone and called the police.

I babbled, “He’s outside again, and again, and I kept all the notes you said and…” She stopped me and said they will have someone out.

“Oh, do you know how soon, because I have to get my secretaries presents for tomorrow and I just have to run out for a couple seconds because if the store closes and I don’t acknowledge their day there will be some angry women on my hands tomorrow.”

She seemed amazed that I didn’t take a breath.

“Well, umh. He will be there shortly. We’ve been watching too.”

The doorbell rang. I took Trevor to the door with me and saw a young man standing there . I hesitated and then saw him flash a badge in the window quickly.

“Wait a second. Can I see that again?”

He looked at me like I had asked him for a million dollars, but showed me his badge again. He was dressed in plain clothes, jeans and sneakers and expected me to think he was a cop!

I opened the door, looking him straight in the eyes.

"Hi. Officer Johnson. Is that his car over there?"

"What, is this a joke? Okay, I won't argue."

"Could you stop being so feisty? I'm here to help you."

"I am going to have to go talk to him to see what his story is."

I stood and watched him walk to his window. Shortly thereafter, the car drove off. The police officer returned.

"Well, what happened?" I asked anxiously.

"He said he was waiting for someone and I told him he needs to move on. He knows he is being watched now. If he comes back, call me. We will be watching."

He handed me his card- Officer Harry Johnson.

"Do you have a log of dates and times that he was seen?"

He sat down and looked through the data. Very complete. This will help."

I let him out and locked myself in. I thought to myself, this is becoming interesting.

Chapter 27

The morning air seemed extremely fresh today as I waited for Jan on the front porch, presents in hand for the girls at work. I said my usual "Good mornings" to the other tenants, especially to Mike. He was a cute thing as I told Jan. Reminded me of one of the drug reps that frequented our office. He always saw me come and go, and run here and there, never slowing down. He probably wondered what the hell my problem was. Does she belong to the fire department now or what? Funny, I didn't even seem to exist before when Peter … Ahh, never mind. I couldn't explain to anyone, partly me, partly the hush, hush of the police force, how hectic my life had become. I looked out of the car window and noticed a pile of boxes on the front porch across the street.

"Looks like someone's moving in." I said to Jan, still looking out the window. When you have lived in apartments this sight always rang a bell in your mind.

“Oh, you wouldn’t believe my evening!” I summarized the evening’s police story to Jan. She shook her head and smiled.

“Oh yes, I would believe it. Ellen, don’t joke around with this, get serious.”

That’s the last thing I wanted to do.

“Yeah, Yeah.” I mocked.

“Ooowee baby. Look at those tight ends!” I laughed as we passed by a group of college jocks on the football field. Jan just smirked and laughed out loud.

We finally arrived at work. I presented the girls with their Secretary Day gifts and they graciously thanked me. I appreciated all their hard work and commitment to the company.

Roman and I always had a moment of tender smiles and quick jokes at work which made each day special.

“You’ll get your Secretary’s Day present later.” he whispered. “Oh, wait. You’re the boss, that’s right. I guess I have to be extra good.”

“There’s always room for improvement.“ I smiled. Those words were etched in my mind from Peter, but somehow, now as I spoke the words, it was funny. Roman laughed not knowing what they really meant to me deep down.

“See you tonight?”

“You bet!”

This particular evening was special with Roman and I. With open arms and a bottle of wine in hand, he greeted me with a smile, and a kiss, and hug. I never got tired of it. He opened the wine and as we drank I opened my heart up just a little. I thought he probably wondered why I didn’t have a steady boyfriend or something. As we layed in bed he listened to part of my story and I suddenly realized that I was babbling away.

“Why am I telling you this?”

"It doesn't matter. I'm a good listener and I am glad you feel this comfortable with me to share your secret, your hurt". "Someday I will tell you mine." He brushed my hair back and kissed my forehead and nose, and then passionately kissed my lips pressing his body to mine. And we made love.

"You're so much fun to be with." he whispered to me.

Nothing mattered at these times with Roman. I never felt that he would hurt me because we both just wanted to enjoy life and have fun. We always did without any second thoughts.

Jan sometimes mentioned otherwards, but I always assured her that "Girls just want to have fun!" And I was. Our times together were only a dream, a movie. "Enjoy every moment while it lasts!" was my motto. I don't think Jan believed me. She thought I would get hurt again.

Chapter 20

This was my big weekend! The weekend that I picked up my car. Jan and drove out to my parents early that Saturday morning. I think I drove her nuts with my excitement. Dad was waiting at the door.

“You know, I think you can handle this from here, Ellen. You and Jan can go pick up the car.” he smiled. I hugged him thankfully.

“See you soon.”

As soon as we arrived at the dealer I saw it! I jumped out of her car, and smoothed my hand down the gold Chevy’s hood.

“Well, what do you think?”

“Good going Ellen!”

The salesman, Ken approached us. “Well it is all ready to go.”

A few signatures and off we went. We spent a little time with Dad and Mom, test drove the car a bit, and before I knew it I was driving home in my car. My car! God I was in heaven. It handled well and gave me a smile from ear to ear just knowing that, yes, I bought this for me. Just me! Jan followed me just in case. Finally we pulled up in front of my apartment and admired it for awhile.

"Jan, really, what do you think?"

"It's great. It's fabulous. You did it!!"

I was so good at making snap decisions now. Just me! I want, and I will get, and I worry about me for a change.

Felt just great!

Chapter 28

Phone calls seemed to get worse. I answered the phone, and ”click”, no response. I seriously started thinking about moving as Jan had suggested several times, but it just was the attachment to my apartment, the home that I made of it, and just simply to be honest, holding on to memories. Hoping that …. Well, I did think about the good times.

The evening was gorgeous. Warm with a light breeze. So I sat on the front porch steps enjoying the summer evening, contemplating my next adventure. I decided to walk down the street to the local bar, maybe have a drink and be amidst a crowd. I walked in confidently, took a seat at the bar, and ordered a drink. It never dawned on me that being there by myself was peculiar.

The older gentleman nearby glanced at me and smiled. I returned the smile.

“You waiting for someone, honey?” he asked.

I looked at him hard.

“No.” I responded.

“Well, usually…, he stopped mid sentence and cocked his head to one side shrugging his shoulders.

Joe was his name. He stopped in after work for a quick one before he went home. Joe worked for the post office and said he frequented the bar after work a few times. Nice place he added, but gets too loud later in the night when the young ones come in.

We chatted about the weather, sports, cars and then I realized it was getting a bit dark out and I’d better get back home.

“Be careful now. There’s a lot of nuts around”.

“Oh, believe me, I know.” That certainly was an understatement. “Bye. Nice meeting you”.

I started walking home. I really enjoyed that talk I thought to myself.

As I rounded the corner a strange shadow appeared.

“Hey baby! Can I come with you!” a slurred voice called out.

I kept walking , not looking back, not responding, and heard his footsteps behind me.

“Why not. We could have some fun”.

He kept repeating himself and falling over his feet. I was almost home and he was pushing his luck. I felt a tug on my arm and I pushed him away. All I could remember was seeing red, as I turned around, and my foot raised for the great slam (you know what I mean, where it hurts). I stopped and ran to the house astonished by what I had done. He staggered, swearing down the street back towards the bar.

This is when I first realized that my temper could flare up in a moment. I read and heard of people getting so mad that they saw red, but until now I only thought that was a colorful expression. Locking the door behind me, I shook. My God, what did I do. I called Jan.

“What’s wrong?”

“I just … “. Jan started laughing in the middle of my story.

“Don’t worry. He’s not going to be bothering you. He probably went back to the bar to ease the pain. At least I know you can take care of yourself.”

And I did feel that I could take care of myself for once.

I slept soundly that night.

Chapter 29

I heard the phone ringing and I opened my eyes realizing it was morning again.

"Hello."

"Hi. Can I talk to Peter?"

"Who? "

"Peter."

"There is no one here by that name."

"I'm sorry. Thank you."

They hung up and I layed in bed feeling numb. Wondering who would be calling.

"Ellen!" I shouted at myself. "Get up out of bed and start the day. It looks great outside."

A lot of times yelling at myself did a lot of good. Getting up early became a routine. I did not want to miss anything.

Working out at the Nautilus Club became an everyday habit too. It felt good and it filled in a lot of empty moments. I usually got there early, sometimes even before they opened. It was a typical Saturday morning, except that there was so much on my mind. I got myself together and started driving thinking that it would settle my mind, clear it out. I tried to workout and ignore everything and everyone around me.This time I was wrong, it was all still there. The thoughts of Peter.

I finished and left quickly out the door hoping to avoid any more Peter thoughts. Throwing my bag into the car, I took a deep breath and started the drive back home. All of a sudden, I saw flashing red lights in my rear mirror. Glancing at the speedometer I saw a big 50 gleaming at me. Oh my God! What am I doing? I pulled over and rolled down the window. The officer walked towards my car and leaned on my window.

"Hi." I smiled.

"Mame, do you know how fast you were going in a 35 mph zone? I looked at him grimacing and thinking, "Please don't call me mame."

"Oh, God. Wow! I am so sorry. But I worked out and I thought I would clear my mind, and then I went to the Eagle and got a present for my dog. You know he's going to be 9 years old and look isn't this a really cute toy and it really didn't cost that much and wow, I'm really sorry. " I rambled on as he looked at me.

The office looked at me and smirked, scratching his head. "Please, just slow down. Alright "

"Yes.Thank you. Have a pleasant day."

I couldn't believe he did not give me a ticket. I talked my way out of a ticket. I kept watch on the speedometer and my lead foot all the way home.

As soon as I entered my apartment I heard the phone ring. Anymore, with the anger inside of me, I didn't hesitate to answer.

" Hello!!" I bellowed half out of breath.

" Ellen.This is Mom. What's wrong?"

" Nothing. What's up?"

" When are you coming home? You are coming home tomorrow?"

Oh no. It's THE BIG HOLIDAY. I froze. My first holiday alone. Memorial Day. This holiday, Peter always showed up with me. It was definitely going to be rough. Mom and Dad figured it out, and Julie and Dave knew. Now, I had to face the rest of the family.

"Ellen are you listening to me?"

"Oh, I'm sorry. Yes, of course I'll be home tomorrow. Is it okay if Trevor comes?"

"Sure. If you want to stay that's fine. How's the car?"

"Great Mom. Great. I'm so happy with it."

"Good. Now be careful driving home. See you tomorrow."

I set the receiver down and sat down with a blank stare on my face. My mind started talking to me.

"Ellen! Get a hold of yourself. You're under control. You can do this."

"Rring."

Again! I thought to myself.

“Hello.”

“Hi. What are you doing?“ It was Roman.

“Just got home from working out.”

“Good girl!”

“So what do you have planned for tomorrow?”

“I’m going to my parents, relatives, picnic and stuff. You know.”

“Yeah, me too. My Mom has been cooking all day.”

“All day!”

“This is the big family Ukranian beer picnic, family get- together." he laughed. “I’ll call you tomorrow. Want to get together. Okay?”

“Sounds like a plan”.

That was Roman. Short, sweet conversation, a quick okay. It never was in his same sexy voice. It was just okay, bye,click and poof he was gone.

My smile, and I mean actual smile, ear to ear grin, stayed on my face for a long time. I got ready for tomorrow with it, I woke up with it, and drove to my parents the next day with it.

As I arrived at Mom and Dad's house, I realized it was early enough that no one had arrived yet. It always seemed like everyone took so long to arrive, except for today. Time went awfully fast.I Helping Mom with the final holiday picnic touches before everyone arrived, I heard Trevor bark as a car pulled in the driveway. I kept taking deep breaths and reassuring myself that "yes I was under control" and it would be alright.

"Mom, do you need anything from the store? "

"No. Why? Where are you going?"

"I just got to take a drive."

This was hard. I was getting nervous and Mom didn't understand. She looked at me confused.

I got in my car and drove, and drove, and finally parked. Cars passed and glared at me. I mimicked them saying,"Oh look there is another crazed holiday person. They probably thought I was holiday drunk or on drugs. Yes, I admit, sitting in my car alone, looking in the mirror, talking to myself was definitely bizarre. But, I never claimed to be normal !

I looked in the rear view mirror and smiled at what I saw. Great tan, beautiful new hairstyle, nice clothes, car! Oh yes honey, I made it out of the great depression !!. Roman will never understand what he did for me. How he helped me. Now it was my turn to face the world, and my relatives (which was worse).

Chapter 30

"Where did you go ?" my Dad mumbled.

"Oh, nowhere and somewhere." I smiled. "Where's everyone?" I questioned as I looked at all the cars parked in the yard.

"Porch. Want a drink?" he asked grinning.

"Yeah, please." I hugged him.

"Feel better? " Mom asked.

"Can't you tell Mom?" Great". She grabbed my hand and squeezed it gently.

The hellos were fine. It was a normal holiday picnic. Tons of food, drinks and questions. I was relieved when I saw Tom, my cousin and his girlfriend, Dorothy. Dorothy looked at me.

"Where did you get that tan?"

"Pittsburgh. Don't I wish I went on vacation." I rolled my eyes.

I looked down at the picnic bench and up at the porch filled with aunts, uncles and family. I was in my own little world and Dorothy and I sat down at the picnic bench across from each other.

"Drink Dorothy?" asked Tom.

"Beer is fine." she replied.

"What are you smiling about? " she asked.

"You look fantastic. How's it going ?"

"Great." I smiled again. "I'm really enjoying myself. It took awhile, but here I am."

Tom returned with her drink and sat down beside Dorothy. I looked across the table and smiled while flashbacks drew my mind wandering.

Why, I thought to myself. Why did Peter do this to me? Why did God do this to me?

I looked at Dorothy getting irritated with Tom's silly teasing. Her face drawn in, no smile, furrowed brow making her look older and older. And I thought, "Oh God, is that how I looked!" I apologized to Dorothy secretly. I excused myself to the ladies room and looked in the mirror. I saw a reflection of a person I had not seen in years. Smiling, cheerful, self reliant, and ever so more confident, something that I had not seen in myself for a lot of my years. I guess it was from that very moment I forgave Peter for what he had done. It seemed that somehow I lost me for a while and clung on to the" we part". I was a whole person again. Maybe this time I was ready for a we.

I laughed at the philosophy and rushed out of the bathroom thinking I spent hours in there. But, I really was not missed.

"So, what's up?" Tom questioned.

"With me?" Oh nothing much."

"Oh come on.There has to be.You're always up to something." he laughed.

"Come on. Everything is ready!" called Mom.

"What can I say Tom?" as we arose to join everyone else. " Life is never boring in my house."

We all laughed, but Tom seemed to be concerned.

As we climbed to the porch steps to join the family, Uncle John arose from his usual seat.

"So where's Peter?"

I froze at the top of the steps, shut my eyes and said nothing. There was silence. I felt like a hundred eyes were on me.

"John, come and eat. It's getting cold." My Mom saved me. The noise commenced.

He never got an answer. No one did. Nor did I.

My sister Julie and Dave kept the conversation rolling and humorous. I thanked God when dinner was over.

"Mom! Dad! I've got to go. Okay?"

I started feeling very uneasy and very lonely. I pleaded with them to not ask questions, pressure me. I had to escape. That is what it was. A bad situation. Time to go. I knew I better start now on goodbyes. Sometimes they could last an hour. I packed up Trevor and after all the hugs and kisses, we settled in the car.

"Sure you don't want to stay for the weekend?" Dad asked.

"Thanks Daddy. I will call. I promise. I love you."

As soon as we reached the end of the driveway I felt relieved. I did survive it. A tear fell from my eye. I don't know why. I brushed it away and drove home.

Chapter 31

This was the famous holiday truck load when I arrived home. I tried to get a parking space close enough to unpack all the stuff Mom sent me home with me. Across the street was the closest this time. Oh well, we will manage. First, Trevor needs out and in the backyard. Three more loads. Not bad.

As soon as I closed the apartment door, the phone rang.

Rrg!! I ran to the phone thinking it had to be my parents still worried that I made it home safely.

“I like the way you bend over that way. I like it alot. I’d really would...”

Click. I hung up and sat down.

Rrg!!

“You are a really very ugly person you know.” a female voice laughed. “You lost!! Ha ha! “ Click.

I sat there with no tears, no anger, but hyper.

Rrg!!

"Hey, I've been trying to reach you all day! You need an answering machine or something."

"Roman! Hi! How's it going there with the family? I just got home."

"Boring. Want to go for a ride somewhere with me?"

"Yes. Oh yes !"

"Be there in 15. Okay?"

"Okay."

I closed all the calls from my mind and touched up my makeup. What timing. Great ! A negative with a great positive.

Roman was on time and I could not believe how we matched. White clothing on tans, white Vet, sunroof ,sun and fun.

"Let's go to North Park."

"I just came from there." I looked at him inquisitively.

"Well do you know a faster way? Which way did you come?"

I directed Roman. He frowned at me.

"This is long."

"Sorry. You asked." He grasped my hand and squeezed it tightly.

"I'm not mad, I just wanted to be there already."

Finally we made it, put the top back on the VET, and Roman pulled out a blanket spreading it on the ground. The sun was setting, but it was a beautiful warm evening. As we laid on the blanket we shared our day's events.

"Dad did not like my outfit at all. I either heard pull it up or pull it down."

"Oh, I like it. You look great, but you always do." he rubbed my leg." You cold?" He pulled the blanket up around us.

"Now this is comfy. Let me rest my eyes for a bit and we will head back okay?"

“Mmm. Whatever.“ I whispered, enjoying his warmth.

It started to darken so we packed up and headed for home.

“We’ll go my way this time.” he said sarcastically.

“Yes sir. You are driving.”

He headed back and I knew we were in for construction detours, but I kept silent and smirked. As we approached the rocky road he bitched.

“Your way may be quicker, but mine was a lot prettier.”

“You’re right. Somehow you are always right.” he laughed.”Never thought you were an airhead!”

“Thanks Roman.”

We made it to my apartment. We made love. We made sense.

Jan kept saying, “I think you’re getting too involved. I don’t want you to get hurt again.” No Jan, you don’t understand. Roman can’t hurt me. I know it's just a dream. I'll wake up one day and it, the fling will be over. But I know I will always have a friend. I know that.

"I don't know, be careful." she would say.

Jan could never accept it, or accept the idea that whatever he wanted to be with me, I wanted to be too. I wanted to stay in the dream as long as I could because what Roman did for me was so phenomenal..

Chapter 32

I was off on vacation the rest of the work week. I just needed this time to do nothing. Roman didn't know.

"I'd better let you get some sleep."

"What for? I don't have to go anywhere tomorrow."

"What! You're off?"

"The rest of the week."

"You little shit. You didn't tell me."

"You didn't ask." I grinned.

"Got plans?"

"No. Just staying here for some R & R, and maybe some more R, if he is not too tired."

We laughed as he wrestled me on the bed.

"God, are you sure you are older than me. How about tomorrow, and Tuesday, and Wednesday, and Thursday and…"I"ll miss seeing you at work. You miss me?" he asked looking into my eyes.

"Maybe I'll come in and serve you breakfast." Yeah, right! Okay! We"ll start rumors. I'll surprise you."

"See you tomorrow night. Good?"

"Good!"

It was 2:30 am, but I was still wide awake. I made myself a stiff drink and pulled the phone to the couch and picked up the receiver. As I listened to the dial tone, it sang out Peter's number. I dropped it as though it were a fire burning my hand. It layed humming on the floor and I laughed as those famous words I screamed at Jan entered my mind, "I'm going freaking nuts." Was I ?

I put the receiver back on the phone and it instantly rang like magic. Retrieving without hesitance I listened.

"Have a good time tonight? " a slurred husky voice whispered. I listened . Silent music in the background and a female voice began to laugh. The same female voice as before.

“Hope you didn’t bore him like you did Peter. Loser!“ she shouted and slammed the phone down.

The words echoed at me in the dark. I gulped the drink and threw the glass at the wall shattering it to pieces. But, I never cried anymore, anger just welled up. I went to bed in hopes it was only a nightmare.

Chapter 33

I awoke early, 6:30 am, and thought I would go to work out early. Then maybe for some sun, and fun, and quiet. The morning was beautiful once again. I decided to not let anything bother me today, but somehow in the back of my mind I knew life was never going to be that dull. As I pulled into the Nautilus Club I always heard myself saying, "I wonder if Peter will be here today?" Then I quickly put the thought in the side pocket of my mind. As I worked out and remembered Peter telling me to do more of these leg curls, remember form, remember form, and counting reps, I became mesmerized in my counting and staring in the mirror. Good, good, keep that form, get that anger out.

"Boy, you sure are serious about your workouts." a voice from beside me commented.

I looked to my right and smiled.

"Well, if you don't do it right, you don't get the job done."

"Sounds like you had a good instructor. Who was your instructor?"

I laughed. “A friend. A friend, and myself, and a lot of stress.”

“Sure looks like it’s working for you. I just joined about a month ago.”

“Well, keep at it! “

I stopped the conversation. I abruptly moved on to the next machine and he followed, but the conversation diminished. After I had finished, I felt great and it was only 9 am.

“Hey, see you later. Have a pleasant day.” I called to him as I did my last rep.

The “pleasant” started at work with my coworkers after they changed the name of our South Hills office to Pleasant Hills office. I continually corrected co-workers jokingly. It’s Pleasant, it’s pleasant. Roman and I always laughed about it privately when we were leaving work and yelled down the hallway “Have a pleasant day !” and he would return with “Have a pleasant evening!”

God, things were going good.

I raced home and got ready for a relaxing day of sun and fun in the park. Tanning lotion, my writing (I always loved to write), pen, something to drink. All set. It was around 11 am and hot. Good ! Good, I said to myself. The park is 5 minutes away and would be quiet. Kids still in school and the major part of the working world gone, it would be quiet. I pulled into the lot beside the park and walked near the tennis court fence. Spreading a blanket and sitting down I felt peaceful, alone, but didn't feel lonely. The warmth of the sun embraced me and I felt instantly relaxed. I only opened my eyes a bit for a few passing strangers.

That's how the first day went. Peaceful. Around 4 o'clock I packed up and headed home. As I drove something felt funny, like I was being watched. Parking in front of the apartment I noticed the "House For Sale" sign around the back. Maybe I'll go. I walked into my apartment and was greeted immediately by Trevor asking to go out. I let him roam a while out back. I cleaned myself up and headed for the sale, if for nothing else for the company.

The people were receptive. John and Sarah welcomed conversation. They were a newly married couple, her second marriage, trying desperately to rid her life of some old memories. I understood completely. As we chatted she mentioned her hatred of phone calls.

"Yeah, I got two answering machines, the best thing I ever got. "One was from a wedding present and one she got from her ex.

I told her about my problems with calls.

"Why don't you look at this one. It will help you. Come on inside."

I was amazed at the ease in making new friends and their welcoming arms.

We walked into the house and I saw the familiarity of the packed boxes. Glancing around the spacious house I thought of my dream to have all this space. Peter and I had just looked at a house before he left and it brought back memories. I spaced out a little with my thoughts.

"Well, here it is. Not great, but it works."

My quick judgement said yes.

"How much do you want for it?"

"Oh, just take it. I know it will help you. I get what you are going through"

"Sarah, thanks so much." Good luck with the move."

"Got to go. Have to meet my friend John tonight."

I ran home, took a shower and called Jan as I was putting on my makeup.

"Jan. Guess what I got today?"

"Hey. What's up?"

"An answering machine."

I told her about John and Sarah, my new friends and the deal they gave me.

"Great! Where are you going tonight?"

"Out with John for drinks and lord knows what will happen."

"Talk to you later. Enjoy work."

"Okay have fun !"

Rrg!!

"Hey sexy. Want company?" I smiled at Roman's voice.

"Yeah, later is fine."

"Our usual. I'll bring something okay? Elevenish? Good?"

"Good".

It was always good with Roman.

Two dates in one night! Well, I'll manage.

John arrived early as usual which was good tonight. We went to our usual place,The Point , restaurant bar. It was quiet and relaxing (except, I was always hyper), and we discussed things, and nothing, and laughed.

"John, I have to meet a friend at 11 okay?"

"Yep, good cause I have work early tomorrow anyway." Just wanted to see you."

I smiled and we laughed. Don't know why. We just always laughed.

We had a few drinks and I thought, God rush home, say good night, change clothes.

You know there is a different dress for different people. Roman was definitely a different dress code. Sexier, more relaxed. John, more subtle, subdued. If I thought about it, that sounded bizarre. So, I tried not to think about it and just did it.

We arrived back at the apartment and John walked me to the doorsteps.

"John, thank you so much. You shouldn't let me talk so much."

"It's good for you. Call you later."

"Okay. Till tomorrow."

I opened the apartment door and glanced at the clock. 10:35. Oh no. I panicked.

In clock time I dressed and let Trevor out and in.

The doorbell rang. I ran to the door and stopped abruptly before opening. Puffed my hair, straightening my clothes and took a deep breath. I made it! Must have set a record.

"Hey." I smiled, embracing Roman.

"Umm. Good hugs. Hi Trevor."

Trevor sniffed at his pants and wandered away. He liked Roman and felt as comfortable as I did. I pulled two glasses from the kitchen cupboard and Roman opened the bottle of wine.

"Thought we would try this tonight. Red okay?"

"Thank you." I said as he sat down and handed me the vino, pulling me onto his lap.

"To tonight! Let's go into the living room."

Roman always made me feel like I was in a movie. Said the perfect words,treated me like royalty, and he loved to give me ideas on what would look great on me.

“Go shopping with me Roman. Help me pick out some outfits.“

“Sounds like fun! How about tomorrow? I’ll be off at 12.“

“Yeah.”

“Hey. Guess what? Remember you said I needed an answering machine or something?” I said snottily in his little boy tone.

“Did you get one finally? Wow. I’ll have to leave some messages for you.”

“Hey, I told you about what was going on with those bizarre messages?”

“You did get one, machine, right?”

“Yes.”

“Good.” he whispered. He grabbed my glass and kissed me passionately. He stood up and grabbed both our glasses and disappeared. I stayed seated on the coach as he reentered the room with full glasses.

"Next." he whispered.

Roman reached down putting his arm around me, picking me up, and carrying me into the bedroom gently. Laying down we embraced and he stared into my eyes.

"Glass please." he asked, holding my hand up. We talked and talked. Clinking our glasses, the wine spilling onto each other, we tasted the sweetness on each other's skin. We made love until early morn.

"Didn't surprise me at work today. Missed you." he commented.

"Only Tuesday, you better get some sleep." I grinned. "You never went shopping with me before. I'm a terror."

You just try on what I pick out. You have good taste anyway. As a matter of fact, we are starting to look alike, you know." Roman laughed. "I got to go. See you tomorrow. 12:30? "

"Of course. You bet me I couldn't work out all week. Bet you an outfit on that ?"

"Deal! See you!"

We embraced, kissed and I awaited the next day.

Chapter 34

I worked out religiously, proven by my workout card and body improvements. Roman arrived shortly after 12:30 for our shopping date. We traveled from one store to the next. He picked out the clothes and I tried them on. And I carried home a whole new feeling of me in every package. We packed up the Vet and I glanced at the pile of packages and laughed.

"I guess I did pretty good, Huh? "

"It's your fault. They all looked so good on you."

I laid my head back and shut my eyes smiling.

"It's so nice to have a friend like you Roman."

He kissed my cheek.

"I'll drop you off and see you later tonight. Unless you have plans?"

"Now I do."

"Let's go out for a while tonight. Okay?"

"Talk later."

As we pulled up to the door, Roman hurriedly picked up ninety percent of the packages.

"Guess I can handle these." I joked as I looked at the remaining two on the seat.

Roman dropped my packages off in the living room, hugged me, and said, "Wear this tonight."

"We'll see." I smiled. I had already planned to wear something I had bought prior. Kind of a surprise.

After he had left, I sat on the floor amidst all my parcels numb. I threw my head back laughing. "Yes, I do deserve all of this and more!" I told myself. "Much more!"

Chapter 35

Rrrg!!

“Hello”.

“About time you bought something new. You were starting to bore him!”

Click.

“Damn it! “ I screamed.

I stared in the mirror admiring the new red dress I bought pre Roman shopping spree. Hair perfect. And yes I felt good.

Roman arrived and stared.

“Hey, I don’t remember that. And I would have definitely remembered.”

“I know. This was my shopping spree.”

“Yeah. I like that. Let’s go show you off.”

We headed for a nightclub downtown. It was crazy crowded so we decided to stop elsewhere. Roman suggested a nearby local place. Looked nice. Different.

That's what I liked about Roman. Always spontaneous.

As we entered we realized we were a little overdressed, but it didn't matter. It never mattered. As Roman always said, "If you feel good, you always fit in."

The place was nice, quiet. Small tables encircled the room. He grabbed my hand and headed for the far corner table by the street window. It was secluded and made us feel like we were in our own little world looking down. The crowd was mingling and we made our own interpretations of who was doing what and where it was headed.

"One more drink and let's go. Okay?" I want to be alone with you."

"That sounds nice." I whispered.

Roman grabbed my hand and his glass with the other and whispered something I didn't hear over the room's clatter.

"What?" I asked him to repeat.

"You're such a fine lady. How could…" and he stopped

We kissed passionately not seeing anyone, or hearing any voices in the crowded room.

I looked into his eyes.

"How or why is not important. Roman is. Now is. Now, is alive. After all, girls just want to have fun!"

"And so do guys!" he said sarcastically.

We did have fun. That we did every time we saw each other. Whether it was once a week or 10 times a week. But Roman never realized the problems I was encountering because when we were together I just didn't care. And before I knew it, another night ended with a smile.

Chapter 36

The next morning I awoke into a dismal day. Cloudy. Rainy. I decided to work out and go visit my Mom since she was home. I packed up Trevor and away we went. Driving was a joy, relaxing, and the country air was solemn. Pulling into my old homestead, I let Trevor out and tied him to his favorite tree and headed for the kitchen door. I saw Mom peek out the window and smile.

"Hi honey." she hugged me."I'm so glad you came."

I sat at the kitchen table as Mom poured me a morning cup of coffee.

"So what's up? What's new? How's Dad?"

"He's crabby, and I've got so much to do around here."

"Oh Mom. I came to see you. So sit and talk to me. The work will be here later. Let's have some fun today. Want to go shopping?"

"Well. she pondered. "Well,why not. How often do I get to see my daughter."

"Bullshit! You saw me three days ago. So stop it."

"I just can't get used to you. You are so happy. Different. So independent. My baby has a car and everything. Something's different?"

"Yes, I know. Now drop that. Drink your coffee and let's go have fun."

I looked up from my cup and stared at my Mom.

"Hey Mom, I'm thinking about moving. Having some problems. I need to. So don't be surprised if I call you up one day and tell you I have a new address."

"What problems? What's wrong?" she asked in a motherly concern.

"Nothing. Alright. Just let's go. Accept me and I'm fine. I'm great. I just got to go. I got to move on. There's so much out there for me and I'm going to get it all ."

"What are you looking for?"

“Just peace Mom. And no,nothing is going to stop me, and no I’m not going to sit here and tell you a depressing story. I want to take you shopping and have fun. Let’s go.” I said forcefully.

“Okay!!!”

We had a day of fun and laughter like a bunch of school girls. Mom saw a side of me she never knew. Talking to everyone and smiling. We shopped at several stores, and I knew she was hungry so we stopped to pick up lunch at her favorite Chinese restaurant, Mei Lee, and headed home for more conversation. It was better at home. More comfortable for me at least. Just in case questions came up and I couldn’t handle life.

We sat down and I helped spread out lunch. Somehow in the back of my mind I wanted to just let go of myself and say “Hey Mom! I hurt. I hurt deep inside. Hold me.“ I wanted to cry, but I couldn’t. That was my secret, my trauma and I didn’t, as before, want the pity and sorrow.

Mom interpreted my thoughts.

“Dating anyone?”

“Oh yeah. Some nice guys. No. Don’t expect me to be home with someone. I’m just enjoying their company. I don’t need the aggravation. No one ever had names anymore. It was a date, or he, or we. No names.

“Where from? Work?“ Mom inquired looking for more details.

“Well, yes and no. Here and there I meet people. You know. Some nice, and the ones that are not, I leave on the roadside. Don’t worry Mom. I’m careful.”

“I know honey. I just worry.”

I glanced out the window and saw how cloudy it looked.

“Hey, it’s almost 2:00. I’m going to head out and besides I do have a date.” I laughed.

My Mom smiled.
“Okay. What can I give you?“

She glanced around the kitchen. She had to always pack me up with stuff. Hadn't learned yet that her daughter did not need to be fed. Her daughter can actually survive by herself and I might add, quite well .

"How about.." I paused. "A hug and a kiss.That's it. Okay."

I headed out to pack up Trevor, but he had other ideas and decided to run around. I called him and he darted several directions at one time with a mind of his own.

I sat down on the bench, feet propped up and shrugged my shoulders.

"He'll be right back, just had to get it out of his system."

"Just like you. A mind of his own." Mom said.

"Yeah! Well sometimes change is good. It makes you realize what you got and what you've got to get together."

Mom understood, but she didn't. That was okay. She just had to get used to me.

Trevor rounded the corner at that moment and stood by the car.

"Alright guy. I'm ready."

"Hey Mom. Had a great time. Thanks. I'll be out to see ya."

"Behave. Love you."

We hugged, and she watched me climb into the car and pull out of the driveway. As we drove it got darker and darker, but we made it home in no time

Chapter 37

The skies came in closer and rain poured and poured. Just made it inside and the phone rang.

“Ellen. Are you ok?” Mom worriedly asked. The storm was so bad.”

“Yes. Just got home. All good.”

The lights flickered, and flashed, and okay, power out.

I sat in the dark room with only the light from the kitchen window shining through.

“Oh no! “ I shouted to myself. ”I forgot to do something special for Roman.”

The lights flickered back on. I knew exactly what I wanted to do. I grabbed the phone book to find a florist near work. I dialed hurriedly.

“Warden’s Flower Shop.” a young female voice chimed.

“Hi. Hello. I’d like to send some flowers.” I hesitated. “Oh, wait. Just one. One red rose. Can you do it before 4:30 today?”

"Where to?" I rattled off our work address.

"Oh no problem. We are right here."

"Fabulous."

We went through the formalities quickly.

"What about a card? " she asked.

"Oh, wow. Yes. Something simple, plain card. Just say, " Have a very pleasant day." No signature. That's it."

"Okay. Thank you."

I hung up and put the call out of my mind, but still smiling. I ran around trying to get the apartment back in order, and getting Trevor back in home mode. My eyes kept wandering to the clock anticipating the arrival of my gift.

The phone rang.

"Hey. Thanks!" It was Roman.

"For what?"

"You know. I knew it had to be you. I really was surprised. That was so nice. Thanks. See you tonight? Pleassee." he sung.

"Yes, yes."

"Hey, did you hear about the flood in Etna?"

"What?"

"Turn the news on . Everything is a mess. About 2:30 today."

"You're kidding me?" I flashed the TV on. Cars overturned, houses flooded, trees down, people on the roofs of their cars.

"Oh God, Roman. That could have been me. I just went through there about 2:15pm. Went to visit my Mom."

"Geez. You just made it. You wouldn't have survived in your little car." He sounded worried.

"That is scary!"

"See you tonight okay. Got a patient here."

Click.

I sat in a daze for a moment thinking "hell that could have been me." Damn, I could have died just today.

I ran around the apartment like crazy and ran down to the basement to see if I left my laundry basket downstairs. I misplaced things and sometimes my mind really couldn't figure out what I had done five minutes ago. As I reentered the apartment, the doorbell rang. It was Jan.

"So how's it going, Jan?"

"Oh,you know, the same old stuff. The TV was still on and we both glared at the news flash of the flooding.

"Oh God, that was so close." she said with worried eyes.

Reflecting elsewhere, Jan asked, " So let's see the new machine." We ran to the recorder as the light blinked off and on.

"Hey, you got a call."

I was so excited. Jan helped me figure out this answering thing. We listened.

"Hi. This is George. Just wanted to see if you were there. Nice seeing you in the park."

"Who's that Ellen?" Jan inquired.

I laughed. "Don't know". I haven't the faintest idea. Wrong number maybe?"

"Ellen!!" Jan reprimanded. " Quit taking these things so lightly."

"I know. I know, Jan."

"Hey. Got to go. See ya. You have plans?" Jan asked.

"Yep."

"Careful." Jan added in her motherly tone as she headed back home.

It was about 90 degrees outside now and more humid after the rainfall. The AC felt so good inside my apartment. Time passed quickly. I changed my clothes and relaxed, resting my eyes a bit before

Roman arrived. I thought perhaps I had fallen asleep dreaming when I heard a loud cheer of voices outside. I slid to the front window to see the elderly apartment ladies across the street on their third floor balcony. They were smiling, and cheering, while they waved their white handkerchiefs in the air. Ethel and Louise were the two ladies that lived across the street in the apartments. They were older ladies, in their late sixties or so, and they loved the balcony sites. Both were colorful and of color, and always hung out on the third floor apartment balcony together. Ethel was short and a bit stocky and loved to wear bright colors.Louise was tall and lanky and was a flowery dresser. Cackling and laughing, there stood Ethel and Louise . They were both wiping their brows from the heat. I heard Louise yell down,“ Oh yes, son. Thank you. Have a beautiful day!”

At that moment the doorbell rang out. Roman arrived in his sweats, no shirt and smiling. I opened the door laughing.

“Didn’t know you had a following?”

“Oh, yeah.” he smiled. “They wave to me every time I come over. Quite a duo”

“God am I hot.” He looked me up and down. “And you are making me even hotter.“

I fashioned my favorite tee shirt alone. I smiled.

“Come on in. I got the AC on and some bubbly to cool you off.”

“Hey alright”.

He relaxed on the couch and I brought the bottle of wine and two glasses from the kitchen. I always let Roman serve. It was something he seemed to enjoy with his sensual comments.

We sipped and he leaned over to kiss me. I blocked his way.

“Roman. I’m thinking about packing up.”

“ Where are you going?“

“I don’t know yet, but I got to go. Too much going on here. Gotta move on. What do you think?”

“I think your apartment is cute.“

“Roman. You don’t understand,do you? I’m not joking about problems. Someone is always watching me. Constantly. It’s like that song by Sting.You know.“

“I’ll be watching you.” he hummed, laughing and pulling me onto the couch.

“Hey, you are serious?“

“Yes, damn it!”

“Hey, then move. Are you looking?”

“Well, yes and no. It’s kind of hard with pets. People are nasty.”

“You don’t have a pet. You have a kid. Pampered one at that. Want me to rent you one of my places?” It was like a light bulb lit up in his mind. “ I could sneak over at night.” he smiled.

“Roman.” I grinned and shrugged my shoulders.

I thought about it. My privacy, my life, my dating. Freedom could not put our friendship in jeopardy. But I kept that to myself.

“Thanks anyway.” I kissed his cheek.

“I didn’t think you were having serious trouble. No one seems to be bothering you when I am here.“

“Of course not. You would probably beat the crap out of them.These guys aren’t built like linebackers like you.”

“Well, bet you could beat the crap out of them.”

“Is my temper that bad?”

“Sometimes I see sparks come out of you at work. It’s cute. And you get feisty.”

Roman hugged me, a really big hug, and talked into my hair. He spoke softly.

“You really don’t know who these people are, do you?”

“No.” I said very relaxed and comfortable in his arms.

“You scared?” he held me tighter.

“I go to different points. Anger, rage, confusion, sometimes take it as a joke, and at times even as a compliment.” I hesitated.

“Yes. I’m scared. I guess especially when that girl calls me. I feel like it’s never going to end. Women are the most vicious, much more than men. Men get bored with games after a while.”

Tears started to well up in my eyes. I was glad Roman couldn’t see my face at that moment. He suddenly turned my face around to his and looked at me. My eyes fell to the ground.

“Look at me.” he demanded forcefully.

“I just want it to end. Do you understand now? It is serious.“

“It will be okay. It will.“ he kissed me gently.

“Damn you Roman. I don’t want to be serious tonight.“

“That’s what friends are for.“

I started laughing hysterically. Jan always said that and we made a private joke of it.

“What is this TOP 40’s night?”

“Let’s make some music.” he said.

We did. And I forgot about all the fears in the world.

The night was getting late.

“Hey. I got to go. Some of us have to work, you know.“

He grabbed my robe and draped it around me and held my hand at the door.

“Guess where the rose is?”

I smiled.

“On top of the ice pack unit at work. Borrowed a vase from one of your employees.” he smirked. “Thanks again. You surprised me. “

“That’s what friends are for.“ I said sarcastically.

“See you later. Good?”

"Good."

I went straight to bed with Trevor following. He looked up at me with bloodshot eyes. I thought I heard his mind say, " Hey,what's up with these late hours !"

Chapter 38

Morning arose with Thursday sunshine gleaming through the window. I layed in bed lazily and thought of times when I stayed in bed with Peter. I had a lot of memories, but only thought of the good times and how I really did miss the something that I thought we had. What, I don't know? I didn't want to think about him anymore because it was over. He said that - "It's over." I will never forget those words. Somehow I kept everything to a certain point and then quit. It's here now, gone tomorrow. Nothing is forever. Nothing!

I jumped out of bed and let Trevor out, made coffee (just one cup), and sat at the kitchen table watching Trevor outside. My mind drifted and remembered sitting there the day Peter and I talked. Suddenly I realized," Hey you've got to get out of here now." Mentally this place has good and bad, new and old memories. Keep the new ones alive. I hit myself on the side of the face and then thought," If anyone saw me they would think I had gone out of my mind." But that's okay. It worked for me.

Besides, I am crazy. Crazed people laugh all the time. I must be crazy happy.

I got myself together to go work out. Glancing out of the window, I saw that man again, just sitting there,now in another car. My heart raced. I felt like a sitting duck. Was he going to shoot me, attack me or just aggravate me. I dialed the phone for my officer friend. It rang. I thought of hanging up, but hesitated long enough until I got an answer.

"Hi, this is Ellen. Can I…"

Before I could get another word out, a male voice interrupted.

"Yes this Officer Johnson." I could tell it was you by your number."

"Well, he's still here, but in a different car. "

"We'll be out."

"Well, I am headed to the gym to work out some aggravation. Is that ok?"

“Yes, we will be nearby watching. Give us a few minutes.”

I took off mad as hell.Temper flying. How dare this man watch me, scoping my life.

Damn it!

Chapter 39

I arrived at the gym and got the usual pleasant reception there. I thought about the evening that Jan and I had planned. She would leave work, I would drive, or she would drive out to a new bar, with a lot of new people to potentially meet. I worked out tough, but it calmed my nerves and mind. I headed home for our evening of fun until Jan was ready.

The drive was slower than usual with traffic. As I arrived home and retrieved my mail from the apartment entranceway. I looked down on the little shelf below the mailboxes. Hey this is cute, a little bear I thought to myself. Looked like a promotion so I picked it up and walked inside the apartment and placed my everything on the kitchen table.

I showered and sat at the mirror starting to get ready for the evening. I was happy Jan wanted to go out with me. We always had a good time.

Rrrg!

"Hey sexy. See you tonight, please." Roman whispered.

"I promised Jan I would go out with her for awhile."

"Oh, I really need to see you. Please." he said in a soft whispering little boy cry.

He always knew how to break me. He was good at begging,especially when the ball was in his court. He always managed to retrieve the serve.

I sighed. "I'll tell you what. Meet me back here at 1:00. Okay?"

"Oh, great. 1:00 will be good."

The phone rang as soon as I hung up.

"Hi, this is George. What are you doing?"

"Who are you?"

"You know me. Did you get my present?"

"What present? What are you talking about?"

"Well, I saw you pick it up, the bear. How about if I come over and we can talk."

"No thanks."

"Boy, you are a bitch. I like that. I'd really like to …"

Click.. I hung up.

Rrg!

"You like me to talk this way, don't you ?" I will be over for the bear bitch."

Click.

Picking up the bear I started to shake. He wants it, he can pick it up. I ran out the door to the porch, shaking, and threw it down on the porch steps.

Running in I felt my heart pound faster and faster, and I could hardly breathe. I stared out the window.

The doorbell rang and I froze. Trevor barked running to the back door and then the front and peered out. Thank God, it was Jan. I opened the door quickly.

"Hey, look what I found on your porch." She held the bear up in her hand and I felt my eyes grow as large as a saucer; as if she was holding a knife. The evening sun flickered on the creature.

“Put it back, Jan. Right now. Get rid of it! “ I said forcefully.

“Jan, some guy put it out there and he’s coming to get it. He’s crazy.”

I rambled and Jan listened.

“What are you talking about?“

“This guy put it out there with my mail, and I thought it was a stupid promotional gimmick and then he started calling and telling me what he wanted for it. And then he said he wanted it back. He’s coming here.Oh, God, what’s going on?”

“Calm down. Let’s go. I’ll drive.”

“Jan, I don’t know what to do. I can’t go. What if he breaks in. What if he hurts Trevor.“

“Come on, let’s go. I am not going to let you stay here alone so it’s best we go out.” she assured me.

Before I could finish the doorbell rang. We both froze. Trevor barked and barked, jumping at the door.

"I've got to see who this is." Jan peered out the front window.

"Well, he picked it up. Looks like a strange person.He leaned on the doorbell and rang and rang.

"I'm coming with you." Jan stated sternly.

I opened the door cautiously holding Trevor's collar as he growled.

"What do you want?"

"You." he grinned, turned and walked down the porch steps.

I'll never forget his face. Blond hair, middle aged, bloodshot eyes. He had trouble standing. I probably could have knocked him over, but fright kept me away.

Jan stood behind me.

“Who are you looking for?” she questioned strongly.

“I’m not interested in you bitch. She knows why I’m here.”

I slammed the door in his face and watched him stagger down the steps to his car. He jumped in and sped off. And then, we heard the sirens shortly afterwards in the distance.

“He’s gone Ellen.” she sighed. “ They said they would be watching out for you.”

“You sure. Jan, just go ahead and have fun. I will be okay.”

“Sure, right. Come on, get your stuff. We need a night out.”

I knew she was right, so I grabbed my purse and headed out the door looking ten million directions at once. We got in the car and took off.

“Oh, Jan. What am I going to do? Who are these people?”

"It will be okay. We need to get out for awhile. "

We headed out to Northview and everytime Jan looked in her rear mirror, I jumped.

"What is it?"

"Nothing, just checking. Driving."

I babbled the whole way there.

"What are those lights up there?"

"What lights?"

I laughed. "Oh hell, everytime someone mentions lights I think of the police anymore."

"How's the apartment hunting?" Jan said changing the subject.

"It's not. I swear everyone hates pets. If I don't get a plain no and the phone slammed, then I get the trials and tribulations of tenants with bad animals."

"Soo….It's not going."

Jan just looked at me in silence.

Chapter 40

We finally made it to the bar. As we walked in I stared at every one as if they were a criminal. We ordered our drinks and wandered around the room together. The music blared and I started to feel a little better, less shaky at least. We stood beside the dance floor and watched, and laughed at the people with ten left feet that should not have even attempted to perform.

"At least they are trying. Let's give them some credit" Jan said.

I shut my eyes smiling and shook my head. Jan and I simultaneously looked around us.

"Hi. You two come here often?"

I looked at this man and wondered what possessed those words to slither out of his mouth.

He just stood there smiling. His blue shirt unbuttoned showing his ten chest hairs caught my attention in not a good way.

Jan interrupted my thought. "I've been here before."

"I'm Tim."

“Jan.” she smiled.

My eyes wandered around the room and set back on his staring at me.

“And you?”

“And me what?”

“Name.”

“Yeah.” my mind scattered.” Name, no I can’t give you a name. No.“

I heard Jan giggle beside me and I turned to her. Tim was still smiling and waiting for an answer. Jan and I looked at each other and started laughing. God was I paranoid.

“Well, I guess I just have to give you one. Ah, let’s see. Well how about Joyce.

“Hi Joyce! “ he smiled.

I remained as Joyce for the rest of the evening.

“Jan, I have to head back home, or did I forget to tell you I had to be back by one?”

"No, that's okay. I can't stand this. But why?" she quizzed.

"I'm meeting Roman." I said sheepishly.

"Don't you think…" she stopped short.

"No Jan." I interrupted." I'm not, and you're so afraid that, and no, it's not that way. I enjoy his company and friendship and…" I stopped suddenly knowing what I was going to say Jan would oppose. No it was not the same feeling as I had for Peter.

"Look there's Zennen." Jan exclaimed. He strolled towards us and introduced us to his friends. Over the loud music, conversations, and with his "heavy off the boat accent", I faintly matched names to faces. I watched as Jan and Zennen went to dance and conversed. Jan looked a little tiffed as the song ended and he rejoined his friends.

"Hey, what's wrong?"

"Just a little pissed off at him. He'll get over it." She did not elaborate and I did not ask.

“Oh, it’s getting a little lame anyway. Let’s go.” Jan announced smiling. “ We might be a little late, but I will get you home by oneish.”

We headed out through the construction and rubble and it wasn’t so bad until we approached my apartment. I started getting jittery about the event that happened earlier that evening.

“Only ten minutes late. Do you see his car?”

“No.” It was kind of hard not to see a white VET even in the deadest dark of night.

“I wasn’t looking for that, Jan. I was looking for that middle aged hippie bear person.”

“Do you think Roman left?”

“I don’t know. His loss if he did.” I laughed. I hesitated as I got out of the car trying to look every direction at one time.

“Thanks Jan. I’ll be okay.” I called to her, approaching the porch.

Jan watched as I climbed the last step. A body flung in front of me from atop of the stairs. My heart pounded. I looked up . It was Roman.

"Oh God! You bastard! You scared me half to death!"

He opened his arms and wrapped them around me. I heard Jan toot her horn and pull out. She knew I was safe.

"Your heart is pounding away. Must be glad to see me?" He smirked. "Have fun tonight wherever you two went? You're late. I was going to take off soon if you didn't show." he rambled.

"I'm here!! I never break a promise."

"Let's go in. I need some AC."

Roman never saw me so jittery.

"What's wrong?"

I told him the evening story as we laid on the bed. I felt so relaxed with him I started to doze off.

"You're not into company tonight. Let me just hold you and calm you down."

"Thanks Roman." I kissed his forehead and brushed his hair back. I dozed for hours it seemed, but when I looked at the clock, it was only 10 minutes. I kissed him gently over and over again. He shut his eyes. I stared at him and saw a man's face, and shut my eyes tight hoping the mirage would go away. Roman jerked awake and looked at me looking at him.

"You had me so relaxed. I'm sorry. I zzzed out." he grinned. "That was nice. I never feel that comfortable. That was really special, you know?"

"Thanks." I said softly.

"I've got to go. Have to work tomorrow."

"Wait." Promise me one thing. Promise me that one night you will stay and I can wake up with you in the morning sunlight."

"Umm.. That would be nice. Okay."

"No threats, just a tiny promise, just because. Okay?"

"Yes mame."

And Roman headed out.

Chapter 41

I set my alarm, and decided to work out and then go to the park. Just relax on a nice Saturday. I didn't worry about "my friends" outside or perhaps I just tucked them away on my "do not ponder pile" in my mind. So I headed for the gym once again. I was building strength in both body and mind. This Saturday was different with a lot of familiar faces from the past, but I kept confident and excited about me. After I completed my rigorous workout, I walked rapidly towards the fountain desperate for water.

"Hey. You look great. How's Peter?"

I looked up and saw Jon. Someone Peter had introduced me to awhile back.

"I don't know. How is he? You probably see him more than I."

"You know, I'm surprised you still work out here. A lot of girls I know would just quit because of the breakup or fight or something."

"So you knew and had to ask?" I wanted to say to him, but held back.

"Hey, it's my world too and I can be anywhere I want."

"I like your attitude and you know, you do look great. Keep it up. Nice seeing you."

"Good to see you too."

As an afterthought I turned and smiled. "Hey Jon.Thanks!" I walked away briskly smiling.

I continued home feeling fantastic and rushed to catch the rays.The phone rang, as it did often, and the funny thing about it was that I was not as frightened.

"Hi. What are you doing ? a familiar voice said.

"Bill? How the hell are you?" It was a mutual friend of Peter's and I .

"Good. How are you?"

"Just great. Just headed for the park."

"Want some company. I may stop by."

"Sure. See ya."

I hesitated a bit after I hung up thinking was this good or bad, but brushed it off with an I don't care attitude.

Jan called before I left. I told her I was going to the park and for her to come. Wanted her to meet one of my old friends.

"Well, I'll try if I get a chance."

I packed up and flew out the door, not positive of what was going to be, but to the park first. Hell another adventure, why not.

I made it there with little trouble, and no interference, and saw Bill already waiting.

"Hey."

We spread a blanket and sat with practically no expression or eye contact at first.

I finally looked at Bill and smiled. "A lot of time and a lot of things have passed. I survived quite well."

"Yeah. You are a survivor."

"Ha. Sometimes I wonder if I'm a survivor or just crazy. Things are a lot different."

"You're a little bit different, you know. I was a bit worried about you, but you seem to be handling this quite well."

"Yeah , right. What else am I going to do? Take a bridge.They don't make them high enough for me yet." I laughed.

We both laughed and Bill pulled his knapsack over the blanket.

"Thought you would like a glass of wine in the park. Do you?"

"Yes. A little would be nice."

I watched as he pulled two wine glasses and a bottle of fine wine from the knapsack. Bill always had excellent taste in fine wines. He looked at me, and paused handing me a glass.

"To you!"

"Thanks, to ME!" I smiled.

“Where’s your friend?”

“Oh she said she would stop by if she got a chance. Jan is a free spirit like me.” And just in that moment she appeared.

“Hey Jan, pull up a piece of blanket.”

Bill offered her a glass of wine, but Jan declined.

“Going down to my sister’s for the carnival. You are coming Ellen? “

“Yeah, think so, but I promised, my voice lowered a bit, “to meet a friend later. “

“ Who?” she whispered.

“John.”

“Ohhh! Okay.“ she said with the voice of approval.

We spent time in the park and all chatted formally.

“You have any problems today?” Jan asked.

“No, not yet.“ I said cynically.

“Are you having some trouble?” Bill questioned.

My eyebrows raised .

"Oh just some assholes that like to follow me. Nothing I can't handle. Besides, it was my problem and no use getting more people involved."

"Yeah, only me. Huh! " Jan laughed.

"Well, Jan,my friend, you were just in the right place at the right time."

I looked at the fading sun.

"Hey what time is it?"

" Five." they said in unison.

"Better get going." I said packing up. I stood up and looked at Bill. Need a ride home?"

"If you can?" he said.

"Jan, why don't you just follow me home, I'll change and we can go from there. " I'll drive."

We headed for our cars and as Bill settled in I looked at him.

"Hey, it was nice seeing you. Hope we can stay friends."

"Don't think that's a problem. Is it?"

I smiled and drove onward. Jan was behind me. It was nice to see a familiar face for once.

We entered my apartment and I grabbed some clothes and scurried in the bathroom to change.

As I entered the living room, the phone rang. I picked it up instantly. Bill sat waiting, and Jan was in the kitchen leaving Trevor out. A simple female voice echoed laughter and click, hung up.

"Damn it, stupid damn bitch" I sounded out. I glanced at Bill's surprised expression at what had just come out of my mouth.

"Sorry." I said meekly.

"Male or female?" he asked.

"Just laughter. Let's go. They can talk to the machine."

We headed out the door and I dropped Bill off at his apartment.

"Keep in touch. Okay?"

"Definitely."

Jan and I went to the carnival with her family.

"Hey, Ellen. How's it going?" her brother questioned as he greeted us.

"Good. I think we got somewhere this time. I got smart and they got stupid." He looked puzzled. "Got a recorder and they like to leave messages. So, I turn them over to the special cops and they are pretty interested in what's happening. I feel like Nancy Drew anymore."

"Be careful. You and Jan."

We meandered and I smiled gratefully at the folks, watching them enjoy the carnival activities. It started getting darker and I mentioned to Jan that I had to go. Had to meet John for conversation and drinks.

"Okay."

As we walked to the car, the darkness frightened me as the breeze whispered out faint noises behind us. Jan looked concerned .

"Just checking." I said as I looked behind us. "Not sure if I should have brought a weapon with me."

Feeling my keys between my fingers I held my hand up to Jan. "Think I'm paranoid." I laughed.

"Better safe than sorry."

""No, with my temper I think they would be sorry."

We weaved in and out of roads and as we approached Jan's car parked in the front of my apartment Jan pronounced," Bet this confused him with my car here and yours gone."

An idea struck .

"Yeah, good thought Jan."

"What?"

"They want to play games, well so will I."

"What do you mean?"

"Let me think about it and I'll let you know."

I walked Jan to her car.

"Be careful Nancy Drew." she giggled.

"Always."

I saw her expression of okay as she walked away.

John left a message on the machine and I returned his call. He picked up on the first ring.

"Okay, John. Will be ready in a half hour."

John arrived in exactly 30 minutes and I was three fourths ready. I put on the finishing touches and ran into the living room where he sat petting Trevor.

"Let's go. Get up off your ass! " I rushed him out. He opened the door for me. Such a gentleman. It was nice, I thought.

We approached our usual destination and Harry, the bartender, an older dapper gentleman, greeted me warmly. As he served our usual, John stared at me and we both laughed.

"You know what Harry said the other night about you…"

I stopped him,"Oh God what?" I said rolling my eyes.

"He asked, where is the lady? Bring her here more often. She brings class to this place. Besides we like to look at her."

"That's really sweet John. He's so nice to me."

"Are you still having trouble?" John inquired.

"No." I said quickly.

"Yeah. You are. If I see those SOBs I'll beat the shit out of them !"

"John. Not you, let me do that."

"Well, I'll hold them down for you to finish them off. Okay?"

"No. If I find them I want them. This is my baby."

"You've got such a temper."

"No, just feisty."

We laughed.

"So what happened last night that Harry was laughing about?"

"I couldn't sleep so I came here and some of the guys and I were drinking shots of tequila and watched the sunrise. Sounds weird, huh?"

"No. Sounds to me like good friends."

"Want to do a shot with me ?" John smiled.

"I haven't done a shot …" I contemplated. " Yeah ouzo days. Shots of ouzo. I remember one night my girlfriend and I went out to the Sanctuary Bar and after two shots of that, a friend of ours that was the Entertainment Rep, convinced us to enter "The Wet Tee Shirt Contest."

"Really?" his eyes lit up. "What happened?"

"Well we got up there on the stage and found out that they threw water on you under the poorly wired disco stage." I said forget it! I am not going to get electricuted, but they threw water on me anyway.

My friend and I walked off with applause, and a free tee shirt. No prize, honey." I laughed.

"Should have won." John said. "I was never at that place. What was it like?"
"A dive, but since we knew the owner, Nikki and the bouncers, we always had protection. A Lot of great times there." I hesitated. "That's where I met Peter. " I rambled, and then I stopped suddenly.

John looked at me .

"Yes, John. That's where a lot of our good times started. I'm not saying there were not any bad times. Four years John. But, I'm remembering good times, not the others. Isn't that what life is all about?"

"Keeps a smile on your face, huh." John smiled.

"Yes sir. New and old memories do that."

John and I looked at each other and started laughing. How we got on to these topics I would never know.

"Okay. I'll do a shot with you."

“Harry. Two more and two shots of tequila “ Harry poured generously and layed out lemon and salt. John poured the salt on his hand and handed it to me.

“ Oooh. No thanks. Just a lemon.”

“ Go ahead. It will taste even worse without the salt.”

“I doubt it.” I swigged it down and chewed the lemon making faces.

“Salt?” he asked.

“Just suck your lemon!”

“Stubborn. Oh, so sorry, feisty.”

We were silent for a moment, but that never lasted between us.

“You still care, don’t you?” John asked.

“About the lemon and salt?” I knew what he meant, but avoided the question with a joke.

“No!” he yelled with laughter. My silence said it all. He knew.

“I really enjoy your company.” John said looking at me. “I was hurt too. Two year relationship. Almost married and she backed out. That really hurt.”

“You never told me. Was it mutual or?”

“Ended up a mutual agreement.”
“That’s a little different John. A lot different. “

“Oh, I know how you feel.” he grabbed my hand and squeezed it.

I smiled knowing all the talk in the world wouldn’t get across the differences that were in our hearts.

“Ready to go?”

“Okay.”

“Want me to stay with you?” John asked.

“No.” I said bluntly and simply without hesitation.

“What if that guy comes back. I worry about you.“

“Sometimes I worry about myself, but I’ll cross that bridge when it comes, or take the bridge.” I joked.

John and I left and as we drove home he stared at me.

"What"

"You're something else."

He walked me to the door and hugged me good night.

I went in and sat on the bed. Looking at the answering machine I pushed the button to retrieve my messages. I laid partially on the bed and listened to the messages.

"Hey sexy. Where are you? Guess you are out. If you get home early, give me a call. Love to see you tomorrow night. Hope you had fun. I'll give you a buzz tomorrow." Roman's voice came over soothingly and I smiled.

Beep.

"You bitch. I'll get you back for what you did. F U." My heart throbbed with temper as the machine clicked off.

Stupid asshole. I got you on tape again I said to myself out loud. I got up suddenly and snatched the tape from the machine and put it aside. Number 2. The police should be able to do something with this info. I pulled at my clothes and flung them on the chair beside my bed looking at Trevor sitting in front of me. He looked concerned.

"Trevor, we will be okay. Don't worry." I hugged him ."We'll find a home soon. A new home with a new start." Smiling, I petted his head in reassurance.

"Now, lay down. Time for bed."

Chapter 42

Each morning rose with a new start. Head clear and a smile fixed upon my face. Things were alright. I wondered if Roman was working.

"Rrrg…" Hey! Did you get my message?"

Speak of the devil, I said to myself. "Yes, yes."

"Well… " he paused long.

"Yes, I do, and what time?"

"Let's do something different. Ummh. I'll think about it. About ninish? "

"Good! See ya."

I wondered what Roman was up to, but knew whatever it was it was a good time in the making. It was sun time. I went to the park and spread my blanket in my usual spot by the fence, close enough to watch the little league games. I prepared myself for a quiet relaxing afternoon prior to a fun filled evening. Shutting my eyes I thought, I really do miss…

“Hey, great tan.” a husky male voice interrupted. I looked over.

“Thanks.” I quietly rested my body back down again and ignored additional talk. He walked away either feeling ignored or sensed my uninterested pursuit in utter chatter.

I enjoyed these afternoons in a crowd, but alone; meeting people, but not at their beckon call for attention. I listened, half awake to the cheers and clatter of the game. The daylight seemed to go way too fast. I rushed home and dressed slowly for the evening in a white sundress.

Roman called.

“ Mind if I come early?”

“Like how early?”

“Eight okay?” He knew already it would be. “ Got something for you when I went to the mall. Tell me what you think of my new clothes.”

“Well, okay. See ya shortly.”

Time seemed to flash by and before I knew it Roman was at the door with his hands behind his back.

“Hey, no hug.” I said as I looked up. Curiosity overcame me. He grabbed my waist with one hand and kissed me.

“Come on, let’s go in. Trevor’s waiting.” he smiled.

I hesitated. I could feel him watching me as I walked into the apartment. I shook my head and Roman rushed to the desk. His one hand was still behind him.

“What do you have there?”

“No. No.” he scolded and pulled me onto his lap. Suddenly it didn’t matter anymore. That was enough of a present.

“Do me a favor, ok?” His eyes lit up like a little boy getting his first baseball glove.

“What do you want Roman?” I said in a Greta Garbo voice.

He smiled. “Okay. Wrong question to ask me.”

“No. Come on. Do me a favor. Your dress is really cute, but could you put on these jeans and tank top for me.” He hesitated and smiled at me. “Then we’ll match. I like that on you better. Please. Please.”

“Okay.” I agreed, partially because he knew where we were going and I did not, and partially because I couldn’t wait to see what he picked out.

I walked partially into the bedroom. I glanced at Roman in the living room and pulled my dress off behind the lace curtain entrance watching him patiently waiting. The jeans were a perfect fit, and the white tank top did my tan justice. I glanced in the mirror, turning and twisting to make sure everything was in place. Of course, he was right.

“Yeah. That’s it.” Looks perfect.” he exclaimed as I walked into the room.

“Now we match!” he gleamed. I looked over at the remarkable resemblance and in disbelief that he wanted to match.

Roman pulled me onto his lap and handed me an envelope. I was speechless.

“Open it.”

I ripped the envelope slowly, pulling out a card, and started to read. Roman interrupted and read the corny jokes on the card with me, holding my hands and laughing. It was signed.

“If you’re ever in a bad mood read this and think of me.”

Roman

“I will. This is special.   I like corny. Thank you.“

“Let’s go.” he bounced me off his knee up onto the floor.

"Let's go have a few drinks in that quiet place down the street."

He petted Trevor. We raced out the door, Roman shutting and securing doors, but of course making sure to open the car door for me, and kissing my forehead. We drove down the street and rushed through the bar crowd to our corner window table. Holding my hands he ordered two drinks. I looked at him as the barmaid meandered to the bar for our order.

"In a hurry or trying to get me intoxicated and take advantage?" I smirked.

"Trying to take advantage of you!!"

I laughed as the waitress filled our table top with drinks.

"Here try this. Ever have a Kamikaze?"

I shook my head yes as a lot of memories of Peter came to mind.

"Bet I can drink it faster than you." I joked.

We both took a long sip and I wondered if I only said and did that to ease my mind, or to prove to Roman that in my stubborn, bullheaded way that I could handle myself. I was a lady that had been around, but was in total control. Somehow when a memory of Peter came into view nothing affected me- alcohol, life, anything that was bad didn't exist. I shut that file in my mind and laughed.

"Hey. What's so funny? A little tipsy?"

"No. I'm just amazed by my company and sometimes I amaze myself."

"Well, you are amazing."

"Roman. I never was this person. I'm me. I feel great about being me. You know how I told you how I felt bad about that night I babbled on to you? It really feels great that I am able to do that."

He put his finger to my lips and I kissed it.

"Someday I'll tell you my story of hurt."

Somehow I felt it, thought he would never speak of it. Someday and forever were words not in my vocabulary because I always reiterated to myself that nothing was forever. Nothing. So I lived for today, tonight, and enjoyed it.

We sipped on our second drink.

“Let’s go after these.” he tilted his head towards me and smiled.

“Uh huh.” I responded nonchalantly sipping my drink.

We finished and raced to the ”Bomb“, as he called his regular non sports car, a sky blue Toyota. As we started down the road, I glanced at him grinning.

“Roman. Want to go to the park?”

“Want to?” he slowed down and pulled over.

We both opened doors in unison and walked towards each other, crossing the street. He grabbed my waist and set me on the back of the playground fire engine and he gazed out onto the dark baseball field.

"Penny for your thoughts." I said to regain his attention.

"One night, I would like to bring a candle, a bottle of wine, a blanket, and some soft music. The middle of the field…" he turned and put his arms around me, his voice getting softer. " And make love to you."

We kissed passionately and made love on the back of the fire engine.

"Let's try your waterbed now."

He picked me up and carried me to the car and revved up the engine. Two seconds away ,into the apartment we made love again and again.

I layed in Roman's arms tightly wrapped around me as he opened one eye and stared at my wide eyed look.

"Penny for your thoughts." his voice raised in question with each word.

"I was...I was just thinking that, well somehow I know that no matter where we are in the world, no matter how far apart, I think we'll always be friends."

"I know that's true. We've had too many good times to forget. You're going to go far and reach every goal you have."

I blinked my eyes with some negative thoughts.

"Hey". he grabbed my face in his hand. "You will, you'll see. Don't be afraid of going for it cause you got it."

I smiled and giggled. "Yeah, but what the hell is it? "

Grinning ear to ear we hugged.

"Got to go kid."

"Okay kid!" We embraced to close another evening.

Chapter 43

One more day, Sunday, before I had to go back to work, so I knew I had better enjoy it. I woke up and turned on the Sunday morning cartoons and realized that I had not turned on the TV in months. I got my coffee and settled back into bed. It was a cloudy, rainy day, but still perfect. My thoughts darted from one subject to the next. I was glad that the phone interrupted me.

"Good morning!"

"Good morning to you John."

"Did I wake you?"

"No. Just watching some cartoons and things. I said in a slumbered voice.

"Like what things? You sound kind of down."

"Well , just that kind of day."

"Quit thinking, it's not you."

"What!" I said angrily.

"Hey, calm it. Don't be so defensive. I didn't mean it in a bad way."

I started to laugh and saw John's face in the phone.

"You certainly know how to wake a person. You got me all fired up for a second. I started to laugh. "Just me, John. Nothing taken offensively." I said apologetically.

"Want to go out for breakfast?" he asked.

"No. Don't think so. I need space to myself today."

"So how would you rate your vacation?"

"Has to be an 11. Good fun! Alright."

"Good to hear that. Can... he stopped. "Can I call you later?" he said meekly. "Maybe we could have dinner or something?"

"Umm. Yeah, ok. Call me later."

I spent the whole afternoon playing with Trevor, reflecting on my vacation and what I accomplished as far as I was concerned. Trevor and I decided we did pretty damn good as far as the entertainment and fun category. Now as far as resolving the confusion, aggravation and new home situation.

Well, we did not win any Academy award, but that would resolve itself one way or another. The clock showed a smile at 5:00 pm and I hurried to dress casually for the evening with John. He didn't call yet, but I knew he was a man of his word. By 5:13 pm we had a set date. Our usual place of Sunday enjoyment at The Point was our quest for pleasure and chatter (mostly me the chatterbox). John picked me up promptly and we headed on our merry way. As we sat in the car and I stared blankly out the window, he turned and grabbed my hand.

"A lot on your mind or bored with my company?"

"Oh, John. Just thinking. I guess about a lot of nothing."

"Want to talk about it?" he grinned.

I smiled and twisted my mouth making one of my famous expressions of what are you nuts or something.

"Now, honey, how do you talk about nothing?" I quipped.

"I don't know Ellen, but we are sure good at it most times."

"Yep. Have to agree. I think you are definitely right."

As we walked into the dimly lit bar, we both fought over the same barstool. There was no apparent reason, just thinking alike as sometimes we caught ourselves doing. Finally, John, knowing how I loved to win, conceded and we sat at the bar..

"Are you having trouble again or are you just in one of your feisty moods?"

He laughed and I instantly joined in. Harry broke into our laughter.

"Hey what's so funny, you two haven't had a drink yet." he said in his raspy voice.

"You're definitely in for a treat tonight then Harry. We are in rare form." John looked at me hard.

"What?" I said knowing his mind was going a hundred miles a minute.

"Ohh." he sighed long and took a deep breath.

"Come on. Let's have it. I know there is something on your mind. You don't hide it very well,Ellen."

"And you do John, come on. You tell me, I'll tell you, just like Miss Jane in 'Romper Room'. Right. Turn the tables, change the record."

"Oh,bullshit!" he said nastily. " You do it all the time and…."

"Hey, I am allowed to get away with it." I said smiling a mischievous smile, coercing John. He followed willingly.

"I know you had a good vacation, but damn, I was only a part of it. Tell me about the rest. I know you couldn't have had such a peaceful boring time and have a smile like that. Although, you were pretty grumbly this morning.

"Grumbly. Thanks."

"Yes, grumbly." he said as a matter of factly. "Why don't you tell me what's on your mind?"

"Okay, you want to hear it. Fine." I said sternly.

"Yes, you are a part of my world, but not all of it. You understand, there are others in my life and that is the way it has to be. There is something out there for me and yes I am going to find all of it." my voice cracked and I calmed down slowly sighing.

"John, for four years I was known as Peter's girlfriend. I want to become me again, someone that people remember and say, " Hey, I know her. That's Ellen. Not just a part of someone else. Just me." I suddenly stopped, and stared at John.

"You're getting there. I know, memories, well loving someone is hard to erase from your life. Remember always one thing though. There are people out there that care about you. Care about you alot." his voice softened and a look of seriousness covered his face.

"I know, thank you John. I mean it. But, let me free."

I yanked on my butterfly necklace as John observed and smiled.

"Butterflies are free and so are YOU."

"You got it now!"

I frowned and then grinned ear to ear. " Can we, like, come over to the light side?"

"Is that a commercial or what? You know, you would be good at those. I can see it now. He joked. "Come over to the light side!!" he said with a heavy deep accent.

"Funny you should say that. One of my dreams was to be in commercials. Acting, Hollywood, and all the glamour and glitter. Might try it."

"Well, why don't you. You got it. Go for it."

I smirked and grabbed his watch for the time.

"Got to work for a living." I interrupted. "Someone has to feed the kid. "

"Stop joking. You know you can if you try."

I shrugged my shoulders with a "maybe" and smiled thinking about how I would even begin. I had no idea where to even start.

"John, got to go to work tomorrow." I hinted.

"Finish your drink".

We headed for the car and laughed about nothing .
"Felt good." John stated..

"What?"

"Being with you and talking to someone, well, with a lot of everything going for them and knowing they are using every bit of it to better themselves."

"Thanks, but that's only the German stubborn in me. Kind of natural."

"Looks like you got things back together from this morning." John glared at me.

"John, the attic in my mind was a little cluttered so I kind of straightened it out today. Filed a couple of things away for future use. Yeah, I'm okay."

As we pulled in front of the apartment John grinned as he walked me to the front door for safety.

"Have any trouble call me."

"Don't think I'll need to. I'm a big girl."

"Have a great day at work tomorrow. I'll give you a call."

"Yep."

I headed in the doorway . As soon as I entered the living room I saw the infamous flashing light of the answering machine. Trevor greeted me with a bark and a "can I go outside" prance. I reached for the backdoor knob and saw a shadow, a figure at the window. Trevor barked and bounced against the back panel of the door, and the shadow disappeared. He calmed ,and I stood shaking cautiously letting him run out the door, hoping whatever, whoever it was would just leave us alone. I glanced at the recorder's flashing light, but walked back to the door to let my great protector in to give me support and courage. I apprehensively approached the answering machine and sat down on the chair glaring at the light. Trevor sat beneath me as I hit the button. The voice rang through me like a chilled fall breeze singing out the female laughter and a hard slam of the receiver. I shut my eyes in disbelief that this was really happening to me. As they reopened tears came flooding out. I sat immobile at the old wooden desk, Trevor licked my hand as if to say, " Mom, it's okay.", and petted him for a few seconds more until I could get enough strength to pull the tape from my machine and document what the P-Force needed. Grabbing the Sunday paper, I spread the real estate section across the desk. My eyes still blurry, but I managed to circle a few ads for apartments that seemed like they were in every part of the world. I had no destination. I even thought of taking Roman up on his offer; even if just temporarily. Tomorrow, yes I'll talk to Roman.

It was midnight, but I never did get very much sleep. It didn't matter tonight because it gave me time to do something that was going to make my life easier. Hopefully. Finally, at one am, my body was ready to slow down and lay down to rest until the morning chimed for me to return to my middle class job life. Don't get me wrong, I loved each minute; all the problems, all the people and all the resolutions I would create. Plus, I'd get to talk to Roman, and Jan, and all the other people that enjoyed my humor that compensated for all my personal problems. No one could ever detect what was happening to Ellen. Jan and Roman knew, but they didn't know it all and besides that, they abided by my law of secrecy.

Chapter 44

“Jan. Hi! Good am!”

“How’s it going?” she exclaimed as I slid into her car.

“Okay.” I said unconvincingly.

I looked at her abruptly and announced, “Just let it be. I’m glad to go back to work. Feeling good.“ I hesitated. “Need to find an apartment fast. It’s getting to me. Nothing, but bullshit.” I pulled the paper from my bag. “Working on it. See Jan.”

She laughed at me.

“Keeping my eyes open too. We got to get you out of there.”

As we entered the old job site I smiled at all the familiar faces and clowned around as usual.

“Great to have you back!” one employee hollered down the hallway. “Good vacation?”

“Only the best.” I called back.

“You look great. Must have had a good one.” my employees chimed as I entered the office.

"Sure did have fun." I smiled. "Now I have to work on the next one."

As I opened my briefcase, the police numbers flew out onto the floor. I glanced down and stepped on them with anger. Theresa, my part timer, reached for them, hesitated and looked up at the expression on my face.

"I'll get them, Theresa. Thank you."

"You okay?" she inquired.

"Oh yeah." I grinned. "Just noticed my desk."

I pointed to the pile of leftover work from before vacation, and the additional mountain topping it, and then threw the paper beneath my foot, on top.

"Oh boy. Now I see why you looked so scared." she joked.

I covered that up pretty good I thought to myself. I got to give them a call to see what's going on with these tapes. They have to find these bastards.

I put my life aside and hid in my work, enjoying every minute. The morning always went fast and before I knew it lunch time arrived. Jan called to see if I was free for lunch and I agreed to join her. Approaching the hallway, Roman jumped in front and looked at both ends of the hall. No one was roaming at the moment.

"Hi." he smiled. A group of employees turned the corner quickly. "So how was vacation?" he asked as if he hadn't the faintest idea.

"Just great, great. Like to do it all over again."

As usual the other girls stared curiously and listened intently trying to see what gossip they could pick up.

"Funny how even the slightest wrong word could start a fantastic story." I whispered to Roman.

"That could probably be arranged." Roman whispered back. "How's tonight?"

Chapter 45

"Could be arranged. Need to talk to you anyway."

"You alright?" his facial expression turned to a concerned look.

"Yes and no, but mostly yes."

"Glad to have you back here at work." he exclaimed down the hall." Wasn't much scenery, at least worthwhile to see when you were gone.."

I smiled to myself as Roman watched me head to Jan's desk.

"Ready Jan? Where to?"

We decided on our usual, The Corner Room, which was a nice, moderately priced restaurant around the corner. We both ordered a salad with house dressing and Jan looked at me, looking around.

"Something wrong?" she whispered.

"No. Just seeing who is behind me so we can talk."

"The coast is clear. More phone calls?" Jan asked.

“I got to find a new home for Trevor and I real soon. I think someone is out to get me for something, I don’t even remember doing anything wrong. Or are they just trying to drive me nuts? The joke is on them.” Jan giggled. “ We ought to tell them they are wasting their time.”

I turned serious. ”Same people, different voice. Male and female, but the same. Doesn’t matter, both are getting to me.” I added,” Don’t worry, so far the police have, let’s see, 4-5 tapes. Getting old, Jan.I have to call them today to find out what’s up. Really getting aggravated and you know my temper.”

“Whoa. Sure do.“

Glancing at Jan’s watch I noticed it was time to get back to work. She grasped my hand saying, “It’s going to be okay. We’ll get you out of there.”

We walked back to work in silence. Seemed like both our minds were in gear.

I enjoyed my job thoroughly and never missed a chance to talk to new people or solve a problem expediently. I think playing Nancy Drew in my personal life made my job solving skills so inane. Other employees were amazed by how I could do ten things at one time. My boss was equally impressed, and I was focused. As the day winded down,Roman said goodbye to me with a "I'll see you later." I sat at my desk wondering just how long this fun would last. I was still amazed that Roman was interested in this person, ME.

Jan called around four.

"Ellen there's something here for you. Can you.." I stopped her short.

"I'm really busy right now, can the courier bring it back?"

"Sure, well.."

Involved in my work I was interrupted by Jan entering the door with the most beautiful flower arrangement I had ever seen.

"I tried to get you to come back, but. .."

My mouth fell open and my secretaries begged me to read the card. Approaching the flowers as if something was going to turn this coach back into a pumpkin, I pulled the card from the ribbon and shook as I opened it. I didn't know who, why. It wasn't my birthday. Who would think this much of me. My mind wondered in several directions.

I read the card twice with tears in my eyes.

"Ellen, SMILE and have a Super day."

John

Jan looked at me and I handed her the card. She smiled.

"Who's it from? " they all chimed together.

"Just a friend." I walked to my desk and settled back to work thinking of how much John's friendship meant to me.

“You're not going to tell us are you?” Erin, the secretary blurted out.

“I did. A friend. They are beautiful, aren’t they?” I smiled glancing at the beautiful colors.

As five o’clock rolled around I carried my flowers proudly to the elevator door. Everyone admired them.

“They’re gorgeous.” said Gina, the secretary from the third floor.” I always knew Peter was a great guy.”

I froze and almost dropped the vase.

“They are not from Peter, Gina. But, they are beautiful!” I said without a second thought.

We stared at each other for a moment and I smiled, leaving with no other conversation.

Everything was fine until, well, I heard Peter’s name, and somehow I wished that would have been true. No. It wasn’t. I pulled myself together and came to the reality of someone really caring enough to send flowers to me. As soon as I arrived home, I dialed John's number. He answered and I babbled about how beautiful, how nice, how surprised, but why?

"Because I wanted to cheer you up. I wanted to do it, and don't you always tell me if you want to do something, do it!"

"Thanks John. I do love them."

"Can I see you tonight?"

"Sorry, I do have plans. Okay?"

"Okay. Talk to you later. Glad I put a smile on your face. Maybe tomorrow? I'll call."

I set the arrangement on the kitchen table and stared blankly remembering Roman was coming over early. It was already eight by the time I got through with my evening duties. I rushed to take a shower and dress for a relaxing night. The phone rang at nine and Roman apologized for calling late.

"Power is out here. Okay if we make it later?"

"Like how late?"

"Eleven?" he questioned.

“Okay.” I hesitantly agreed, knowing I wanted the company.

I waited. I read the rental ads and decided to call a few. I shouldn’t have. The no pets, absolutely not, changed my mood and evening. When the phone rang at eleven and Roman suggested an alternative day, my evening was shattered. I told Roman it was alright even though it wasn’t.

“Talk to you tomorrow.” he said. He knew I was not pleased.

Chapter 46

Days at work went extremely quick. The workload evened down to a daily routine. I spoke to the P force and each time they reported to me, but it seemed like everything was not going fast enough. They repeatedly stated that they had a lead, to keep tracking everything that happens, but wouldn't give me details. My temper was worse than ever, especially after a phone call and sighting of a car outside my doorstep. At times I thought," What the hell, why should I bother, should I just get a gun and take care of everything myself? Then I calmed down and realized that would not solve my problems. I wanted everything now and I became more and more impatient. Jan still drove us to and from work. Every night when she dropped me off we would check for that car. It wasn't there. He knew our pattern all too well and planned each day to catch me alone. My life continued with calling for apartments and I was determined to find one this week.

"Hi. I'm calling regarding your ad for the one bedroom."

The man answered intently. I was impressed.

“Do you accept pets?”
“Oh lady. We had a tenant that had a bird once. God what a mess. What do you have?”

“A dog, a small dog, well behaved and …”

He interrupted, “God lady, that bird was a holy terror. I”ll tell you what. Let me meet your dog and maybe we can find something for you.”
“You want to meet my dog? What about me?”

He laughed. “Well yes, you too. Is your dog clean?”

“Just got a bath yesterday.” I was puzzled and felt uneasy about this man’s obsession. Luckily, the call waiting on my phone interrupted.

“I’ll tell you what I will call back in about 5 minutes to make arrangements for a meeting. Your place would be fine.” he said cynically.

“Will let you know.” I repeated knowing full well this was not the place for me .

I answered my call.

"Ellen, get your ass over here right away. How fast can you get here?" Jan was acting very mysterious. "Just get over here, I found a place for you to look at."

"Okay."

I hung up the phone, tied my tennis shoes, and drove over to Jan's apartment. Jan met me as I pulled up in my car.

"Where to?"

"It's the house next door."

"First, second floor?" I asked.

"The house next door. Come on!"

I couldn't believe what she was saying. This was worth all the aggravation of apartment hunting. But my mind wandered, thinking that this could not be that good. I couldn't wait to see inside. I was greeted by an elderly man at the back door and welcomed in.

"I'm Chuck. Place has been vacant for a while. Peg's sister in a nursing home down the road. A woman appeared from around the corner of the kitchen and we introduced ourselves.

"Peg can't see too well. Just had surgery, cataracts." he explained, grabbing his wife's arm.

"This house is beautiful." I exclaimed.

I felt as if I had known them for years. Like an Aunt and Uncle or something, the way they treated me.

"Come on, we'll show you around."

I gazed at the gold walls and gold plastic back curtains on the large living room window.

"Place needs a little work, but solid." Chuck said showing me room by room and smiling.

"You know, we're getting old. Got a place of our own and well, just too hard for us to run back and forth to check the place everyday. Wasn't thinking about renting till our friend next door mentioned it. Leaving most of this stuff here if it is okay with you?".

“May I ask what you are asking for rent?” I questioned, thinking this has got to be way out of my range.

“Oh well.” the Mrs. stopped. “Umh, is $250 alright with you, or is that too much?”

“That’s fine with me.” I said excitedly.

“When do you want to move in? We probably could have some of this junk out of here by the weekend.”

I was astonished.

”Don’t rush yourselves. I have to tell my landlord first, but he already knows I am going to move, so I don’t think it is a problem. “

“We will leave the key next door for you. Okay?”

“Great. Perfect. Thank you.”

Jan and I left and she walked me to my car.

“I can’t believe it. It’s perfect. I can’t wait to tell Trevor. Thanks Jan.” we hugged.

“We’ll talk tomorrow about moving.” Jan smiled and hugged me again.

As I drove home, I wondered how things worked out like this for me. I couldn't wait to get out of my apartment. I rushed to the door and hugged Trevor, noticing the answering machine light blinking. Message one, John. Message two, Mom. Message three, "You stupid bitch. Slow down, don't drive so fast. Couldn't catch up with you."

I laughed like I never did before at that message. I couldn't believe my ears. This man is telling me he could not keep up with me. This man that has been trying to instill fear into every day of my life for months, wanted me to wait for him to do God knows what to me; to my sanity. I kept laughing as I lifted the tape from the machine and replaced it.

" Well, here goes another tape." I said as I placed it in the envelope with my dated phone calls and car appearances. Then, I hid it in my dresser drawer, just in case, so nothing would happen to it in the meantime. I wondered when this game of cops and robbers would end. Shrugging my shoulders at that thought, I set my mind to my new home grinning ear to ear. Boxes, packing, moving, I had to call the

P-force to notify them. They would probably be so glad to hear I was moving out of their jurisdiction.

Chapter 47

I called Jan to thank her again that evening, and thanked her again, and again the next day until she finally told me to shut up. Next step, to call my landlord,Len. Len knew bits and pieces of my problems, but didn't know how serious it had become. Roman stopped me in the hallway that afternoon to ask me what I was grinning about.

"I'll tell you later. Too many people around and I can't let anyone know what is going on just now."

"Alright Miss Mysterious."

To my surprise Jan walked down the hall with tons of boxes in hand.

"Jan! Great.Thanks."

Someone whisked past us saying," Someone moving?"

I stopped quickly. Jan and I looked at each other.

"Oh, no. Just cleaning the house. Great boxes for storage." Jan responded quickly.

Good going Jan, I thought to myself.

“Thanks.” I whispered to her.

As we packed the car, and headed to my place, a thought came to mind. I need to call the P-force as soon as I get home.

“We’ve got to be careful taking in all these boxes. We don’t want your nutso friends to know you are packing. I’ll bring them over later tonight, okay?” Jan said. “Just take a couple in now.”

“Oh, that’s right. How the hell am I going to do all of this?”

“There’s a way. You’ll do it. You always have ideas.” We both laughed.

As soon as I got in and secured the door, let Trevor out and in , I phoned the precinct.

“Hi, this is… “ Before I could get my name out the male voice spoke again.

“Hi, Ellen. What’s going on?” It was Tony, one of my protectors.

"I found a place to move. It's just great, got another tape for you too." I said in one breath.

"Whoa. Slow down."

"Sorry. I just can't wait to get out of here, away from…"

He stopped me short. "We have to take precautions now. Don't want to take a few bad friends along with you, do you?"

"What do I do?I questioned." Find out anything yet?"

"Close, but can't say anything yet."

"Come on. I have a right to know." I sounded aggravated.

"I understand, but we have to do this our way, so quit getting so feisty. "

What? Feisty. I felt my temper rise.

"Listen to me now." he said. "First, packing."

"I know. Jan already told me to be careful dragging boxes in here."

“Okay.” he said as if he couldn’t believe Jan got to it before him. “Okay, #2 . Moving has to be done on the QT.”

“When’s that?” The stroke of midnight or something?” I joked.

“You got it. From what I figure, they are never around early in the morning or late evening. It has to be done this way.“

“Got it. Okay I will keep you posted.”

“Hey, wait a minute, one more thing.” He said firmly. “No new address, no new phone number given out to anyone.”

“Anyone? What about my family?”

“Nope. No one right now.”

“Yes sir!” I practically saluted the phone and hung up.

I was amazed at how fast the boxes filled and how much was left to do. My mind darted in ten million directions. The phone interceded my panic.

"Hello."

"Hi, sexy. So what's up. What's the big secret?"

"Guess what Roman! I found a place to move."

"Yeah. Where?"

"Near Jan. It's a great house."

"What are you going to do with a house?" he inquired.

"Live! What do you think?"

"I didn't think you had enough to move into a house. It'll be empty."

"You'll be surprised."

" Hey, can I see you tomorrow and the next day, and the next, or are you really mad at me?"

" No, I think that's passed. I was just disappointed. See you."

" I promise this time. I am so glad you are not angry." he said softly.

Chapter 48

As the morning grew near I caught a few extra hours of sleep. Trevor and I were exhausted from all of our late nights. I awoke, unusually late for us, and decided to head for the sunny afternoon. All packed and heading for the door, the phone rang. I realized as I glanced at the phone, that I forgot to turn the answering machine back on. Picking it up hesitantly, I was relieved to hear John's voice.

"Hi. What's up? How come you're not in the sunshine?"

"Heading there now, but you stopped me." I laughed. " Something wrong?"

"Nope.Tonight good?"

"Yep! I have a lot of news for you, but I'll let you hear it all tonight."

"You sound excited. What is it? Find an apartment? Getting married? Huh!"

"What the hell are you talking about? Married? What's that shit. I said I'll tell you later." I laughed.

“Okay. Ms Mystery. Go catch the sun and I will see you around 7:30 or so.“

“Right. Bye John!”

“I know.” he mocked. “Say goodbye John. Shut up John.” he laughed.

“Alright smartass. See you tonight.“

I hung up the receiver, set the machine, and flew out the door. The little league was playing their usual Saturday afternoon game . Claiming my usual spot I made myself at home and settled down for a nice relaxing afternoon. Scores of parents set up their sights to watch the kids scramble for the first big hit. Unfortunately, sometimes there was a wait for that event.

“You come here often?” a husky male voice shouted towards me.

I glanced up and smiled, and almost laughed at the man matching the little league outfits.

“Looks like you’ve been coming here a long time. Aren’t you a little old for the team?“

He grimaced and a thousand faces turned to me.

Always got to be a clown in the group. Great tan clown." he smirked.

"Thanks."

The game proceeded and even with all the cheers and screams I still managed to fall asleep waking up to the sight of 4:00 on my watch's face. I scrambled to home,retrieved my mail ,which was the usual bills and junk. Trevor barked as if to say, "Hey mom, where have you been all this time? Hey,I am hungry." I glanced at the clock and saw the shadow of five. I had to get going, I thought, tons to do before John comes. John was always on time. Somehow the tables were turned from when Peter and I were together. Peter was notoriously late. Now, I was always the one running around with someone waiting. I settled Trevor and started rushing around like a mad woman thinking about all the things I had to tell John tonight. I almost made it on time, except for he was fifteen minutes early.

"Come on in John. I'll be ready in a sec."

John followed me and rattled while I put on my finishing touches of makeup.

“So, where are you going this time ?” I inquired.

“Scranton. A big convention. Will be gone a week.”

“Sounds kind of boring. I knew someone from there once. Nice person.”

“What? Old boyfriend?” he asked.

“As a matter of fact, it was. One of those three months and it’s over deals.” I stated. “I got over it pretty fast though.” I didn’t even look at his expression. “So, are you ready to go? Where to?”

“The Point? We can talk there. I want to hear all your excitement. “

“I found a place John. It’s great. The house right next to Jan.”

“Wow. Great. When are you moving in ?”

“Well, I have to pick up the keys first. Soon.“

"Where are the keys?"

"They are leaving them with Jan's landlady. So,I guess whenever." I stopped and turned to John with excitement in my eyes.

"Hey, so do you want to pick them up now. We can drive over before we go out. Anyway you want to see the place, or do you want to wait?"

"Let's go." John grinned and led our way out.

John asked ten thousand questions on the way over.

"You'll see soon enough for yourself tomorrow. It's great."

It took us no time at all to arrive. I knocked on Jan's landlady's door, Helen. She opened it and slowly peeked out with her china doll face.

"Ellen." she smiled." I bet you want the keys to the house dear?" she smiled. "I'm so glad to finally have a neighbor."

"Oh, I am so happy. Can't wait to move in. Oh. I'm sorry this is my friend, John."

“You two going out?” she asked.

“Yes. Just wanted to get an early start on moving in tomorrow. “

“Oh great. I’ll be seeing you soon then dear.”

“Bye.” we all sang.

John looked up at the house. “That’s it, right?” he questioned, scanning the two story house.

“Nice.”

I smiled glaring at the house. John and I ran to the car and set out for a celebration drink . I could not erase the smile from my face. We entered “The Point” both eager to have a first toast.

“I’m so happy. I really am. “

“So, I can tell, and everyone else can too.“ John smiled.

“I can’t help it,John. Finally something is going right. I am so excited.“

John just sat there and laughed.

"Things aren't that bad. Although you're the only person I know that has so many bizarre things going on in their life. A lot of people would have given up by now."

"What's to give up? Knowing my luck I'd jump off a bridge and still survive. Why make it even harder."

He smiled and shook his head. "That's why you intrigue me so much. You don't give up. Your ship could have a thousand holes in it and you'd probably say, "It can be fixed, just give me time."

"You mean my ship came in and I missed it? Damn it!" Our laughter was so infectious that people around us began to smile and laugh.

"Hey, I have a great idea."

"Umm." I hummed.

"While I am away, let's keep a log of everything that happened during the week, and then come back next Sunday to report to each other. Besides, I don't want to miss anything!" he smiled.

"Good."

"Hey, what time is it ?"

"1:12. "

I dug in my purse and John watched curiously.

"Finish your drink and let's go. Can't wait." I said, pulling out the new keys. " I really want to see it when no one is there, you know what I mean."

John nodded and we drove on. As we pulled in front of the house I jumped out and stared at it. John swung behind me and placed his hands on my shoulders.

"This is one hell of a place.Great."

"Come on. Let's go. "

We raced to the front door and fiddled with the keys. It seemed like hours, but we managed to gain entry. John and I roamed around some of the packed boxes and furniture still left to be moved by the owners.

"So what do you think?"

“It’s great. I’m jealous. Needs some work, like paint,but we can get it done.”

“WE” rang through my body like a knife.

“We?“ I questioned John.

He looked at the hardened look on my face.

“What’s wrong? What did I do?” He questioned with concern.

I sat down on the couch. John followed me and put his hand on mine.

“John. There is no we. I still have to find me. I’m…”

“I know. You’re not ready for that yet. I know what the problem is. You’re still not over him. You need your space.“ he said quietly and sincerely. “I’m sorry.”

I stared at the wall. He was saying things that I didn’t want to hear. I wanted to get over Peter and I really thought I was doing great. But, I knew it was true. I hadn’t gotten over him. It hurt deeply. But, being obstinate, I shook John's hand from mine and repeated, " I'm doing fine, just doing fine by myself."

"Show me the rest of the house." John asked, changing the subject.

We wandered around and decided to call it an evening. Driving home I grabbed John's hand.

"Thanks for being a friend."

He just grinned, led me to the door, and kissed me gently on the cheek.

"You sure a friend can't stay with you?"

I smiled and lowered my eyes to the ground.

"I'll give you a call before I leave okay? Be careful." he hugged me.

I watched as John pulled away and wondered why I couldn't feel for John the way he did for me. Maybe he was right about Peter. Maybe …. I dozed off to sleep.

Chapter 49

The next day at work time seemed to be flying past me. I headed for the conference room with piles of undone work and settled myself behind closed doors. As I was starting to sign off timesheets my mind wandered. Apartment, Peter, security, Roman and everything. Quickly I refocused and regained sight of my work, finally getting myself totally involved in the scheduling issues. I was suddenly startled by a kiss on my shoulder, jumping in fear of someone behind me.I turned and saw Roman smiling.

“Don’t ever sneak up on me like that! “ I scolded quietly and smiled.

“I’m sorry, just wanted to surprise you. You have been in here all morning.“

“Yeah, time isn’t on my side. There isn’t enough to fit all of this work in.”

“You haven’t been to your office. Going back soon?”

“What time is it? Why are you being so mysterious?”

I grabbed his watch and saw 10:55 am. "Oh, God. I have to be back for lunch reliefs."

"Hey. See you tonight for sure. Right?"

I smiled and packed up quickly to head back. Roman watching my every step.

Entering the office I threw down all my papers onto the desk while all the secretaries gleamed at me.

"Well, you got an admirer again." they chimed.

They watched as I picked up the tissue wrapped flowers and fondled each leaf. Three beautiful red roses.

"Aren't you going to read the card?" they questioned between phone calls.

Rustling the tissue paper, I tore the envelope open, and read each word carefully, grinning from ear to ear as I hung on to each word.

"Well?" the newest secretary questioned, staring at me. I giggled like a high school girl.

"I don't know, they didn't sign it."

"You know." she exclaimed. "I'm getting pretty sick and tired of this. Since I started working here this is the second time you've gotten flowers. What's your secret?" she smiled.

"I don't know? I said furrowing my brows. "But if I did, I certainly would not be working here. Would have bottled it by now making millions. "

I searched for a vase and set the roses on my desk beside me glancing every moment with a smile. I wanted desperately to go see Roman and embrace him gratefully for his warm gesture. I knew that I could not.

Later that afternoon, returning to the conference room to try to settle back to some serious work, Roman popped his head in the door. Turning quickly from my chair, our eyes met and smiles said all the words that couldn't be said.

"See you tonight."

"I'll thank you later. The way I really want to thank you."

Roman faded out the door. No other words had to be spoken.

As the day sped past and I saw five oclock shine, I rewrapped the roses to follow the noted orders. The note read:

"One because I'm sorry, one because I miss you and one for the table next to your bed for tonight".

The other girls ogled in the elevator at my gift and I held them against me glowing. Jan only had a few words to say.

"You know, it doesn't surprise me. Roman is very romantic. Just don't…" she stopped.

I knew what she was about to say. Just don't get involved, don't let yourself get hurt. But she didn't finish. Obviously she knew whatever she said would not stop me. What she didn't know was that I still had my heart somewhere else.

Arriving home, I ran into the apartment and placed a single rose in each room. One on the kitchen table, one in the living room between two wine glasses waiting to be filled, and the last one next to my bed in my favorite milk glass vase.

All ready and dressed in my black mini outfit, I sat and gazed at the now fully opened rose on the living room table. I wondered momentarily if Roman would really arrive tonight, but my thoughts had dissipated when the door bells chimed. Tonight they sang a different song as I rushed to the door and into his arms. We held onto each other as I whispered thanks into his ear a thousand times. He just smiled at my happiness with his present and led us into the apartment, gallantly opening the bottle of wine with one hand and holding me in his arm with the other. It wasn't working well, so I slid in front of him leaning my body back against his and letting him utilize both hands to serve.

"Thanks." he laughed. " Was trying my damndest, but…"

Picking up both glasses, arms still reaching around me, he kissed my hair and maneuvered us towards the living room. I grasped the bottle.

"Didn't think you could handle everything at once, did you?"

"Hey, you're an independent lady. You can do something? " he smirked as we led each other to the couch.

Roman held his glass up for a toast. "To Big fun!" I followed and repeated. "To Big fun!" Setting his glass down he turned abruptly towards me.

"I didn't tell you, did I ?"

"What? " I looked into his eyes.

"How sexy you look tonight. Very nice. You deserve roses everyday."

I smiled and slightly blushed, but accepted the compliment thinking that, yes, maybe I do.

Roman poured us another glass of wine grasping my hand.

"Getting kind of warm. Mind if I take off my shirt." he smiled already halfway there.

"Guess not. Anything else?" I said with a why are you asking note. He knew I didn't mind anyway. Everything he did was my new attitude. Do what you want to do and don't worry about what other people think. Have fun. And I was, and I did with Roman. I felt like nothing in my life, no matter how bad it was could ever get in my way of being happy. A lot of times, this cops and robbers game tried diligently to do so, but luckily for every bad there is a good and I seriously started believing the song . Except for mine went in three. Three good, three bad. It was a pattern for three months. I joked about it, but when I took a good look, it was scary. I finally decided to stop looking back at the bad and smiling at the good. Roman and I enjoyed each other's company as we always had and closed the evening with a smile and note of yes. Oh yes, we 'll do this again. I often wondered if there would be a next time, but always knew there was not a forever. No commitment as I said to him. Leave well enough alone as long as a smile is involved. Always was, always will be in my heart, and my mind.

Chapter 50

The alarm rang and startled me. I jumped from the bed hoping I could find some way to explain to my landlord about moving. As Jan and I drove into work a thousand and one 'What ifs?" blurted from my mouth. Jan suddenly stopped me and said, " Ellen, just tell him. He'll understand. Don't worry, it will all work out. Trust me."

How could I not trust Jan. She was watching me step by step, putting my life back into order or at least some sort of assemblance. First thing I did as we entered work was to call Len. His answering machine sang out loud and clear so I left a message and my number. Each moment I anticipated his call. One hour had passed. I headed to the office to try to get things accomplished and then finallyI settled in the conference room and heard the phone blare out. Grabbing it on the third ring I heard Len's voice. My heart pounded.

"Ellen. Hi. This is Len. What can I do for you?"

"Oh Len. I just don't know how to tell you. I don't know how to explain the predicament." My voice shook.

"Well, just go ahead. You sound upset. Are you alright?"

"Yes and no. You see all the problems I've had and people bothering me, and memories and well."

"I think I know what you need. "

I was surprised by his statement.

"Len, I'm afraid that I am going to have to ask you if I can move soon. I just can't deal with all of this anymore, and well I'm scared." Tears started to fall from the corner of my eyes and my body shook.

"Look, it's okay. I understand. I think you need to get out. I'll work with you. Just try to stay calm. Whether you want out the end of the month, or first of the month, that is okay. "

"Thank you Len." I wiped the tears from my eyes. "Thanks so much."

“Okay. Be safe, and if you need help let me know.” said Len in a fatherly voice.

“Thanks again.”

I ran to Jan’s desk still wiping tears from my eyes.

“Ellen, are you alright! What’s wrong?” her brows were furrowed.

“It’s okay, Jan. I just talked to my landlord and…”

“And what?” she said.

“He said alright. He will help me.“

“How soon can you…. “ she stopped mid sentence.

“Hey! What’s up?”

I turned suddenly to see Roman glaring at my eyes.

“You okay?” he said as his smile faded a bit. ”Come here into my office.” He grabbed my hand and pulled me into the conference room. I smiled and glanced back at Jan.

Roman kicked the door slightly shut.

“Well. What’s with the tears?”

“Just talked to my landlord and I guess I just feel a little relief. Nothing big. “

“I’m glad you are getting out of there. Want some company tonight?“

“Sure do.”

Roman glanced around and kissed my cheek. I shut my eyes for a moment and tried to hide from my memories, or at least put them in storage for a while. But John’s voice kept echoing, “You still haven’t gotten over him.” I wondered if moving would make it all go away. I knew it wouldn’t.

I carried boxes home with a different attitude that evening. “Hey, like I’m actually leaving, making a new home, and I spoke over and over that I was going to have a whole house before I was thirty.” I finally realized that I did it, even if I didn’t own it, but it was still part of my dream. And I did it! I threw the boxes aside when I got home and got dressed to see Roman. I waited & waited and threw a couple boxes together. Eleven thirty rolled around as the phone rang.

"Hi. What's up?"

"I'm in a really raggy mood. Tonight is just not going well at all. Will you be terribly upset if.." Roman started.

I interrupted Roman finishing his sentence, knowing what he was going to say.

"If you didn't show up. No. Want to talk? " I asked.

"Oh. I got into a fight with the neighbor about parking spaces and it just really got on my nerves."

I listened intently, but in my mind I knew that this was a part of the "we've had fun, but I'm pulling away". I understood because I always knew it wasn't to last.

"Hey. Thanks for listening to me. Are you sure you are not angry?"

"No. I can't be. It doesn't become me at all. See you tomorrow. Okay?" I stopped. "Roman, remember you can always talk to me."

"Okay.Thanks."

Click. Silence.

Chapter 51

I grabbed my purse and looked for my keys. I wanted to just leave, but as I fingered the keys I stopped short, and rubbed the one key that I had completely forgotten about. It was to Peter's car. Oh God, I forgot to give this back. Should I take it back or just forget it? No, I'll mail it back tomorrow, that's what I will do. Yeah, that's what I will do with a note of "I'm sorry, I forgot." As I grabbed a piece of paper to write I went blank. What do I say? "Hey sorry, but I'm absent minded. Sorry, I just wanted to keep a part of you. I hate you. I love you. I'm stupid". My pen went wild and scribbled over everything I started to write like a wild woman. Crumbling the paper I sat back and stared blankly and calmly almost like I was put into a trance. I grabbed a small box from the desk drawer, removed the key from my keychain and placed it delicately inside. I wrote," Peter, I'm sorry I forgot to return this sooner. Ellen" and addressed the box with no return address and went to bed.

Jan arrived on time the next morning as usual and I jumped in. “Jan, I got to go to the post office today at lunch okay?”

She looked at me strangely, noticing my frantic voice.

“I forgot to return something and I”ve got to send it today.”

“What’s that? “ she inquisitively asked.

“Peter’s car key.”

Jan just stared at me with no response.

Work was normal and by lunch time I was dashing outside, box in hand.

“Boy, you’re really nervous about this Ellen.”

“Just have to return it, just something I have to do. You understand?” I said as we approached the window. I told the woman of my desire to send this to this address, certified if possible. It wasn’t that easy as everything turned out to be for me.

“Well, we can’t mail it like this?” she exclaimed.

"Why not? " my voice became testy.

"Too small. You'll have to put this in something bigger."

"Like what?" my voice was angry. All I wanted to do was to get it out of my hands and on its way. But, no, it was not that simple. She looked around her shelves looking at the panic in my eyes. "Here. Place that in this envelope and readdress it."

I sighed and took the envelope from her. Fumbling with it nervously, Jan helped me, and back in line again, we waited, my foot tapping anxiously each step of the way back up to the counter.

"Is this okay now?" I said as our eyes met.

"I'll fix it for you dear. It will be good" she said as she smiled and placed the green certified sticker onto the parcel.

"Thanks for your help." I said sheepishly. "It's just, really important I get this out today."

Still smiling in an understanding way she handed the receipt back to me closing our transaction. I turned to Jan. “On the way.”

“Feel better?” she asked.

“Yes. I’m okay. Just something I had to do, you know, for me.”

Chapter 52

Religiously Jan and I carried boxes home each evening.

“What’s on the agenda for the weekend. Want to go out?” Jan smiled.

“Well, Roman wants to come over, but not till later tonight. Want to go have some fun?”

“Okay. I’m up for some fun!” Jan laughed. “Where to?”

“Anywhere and everywhere. Why not!”

Jan twisted and turned around my apartment through the back alley. She thought we could catch “him” off” guard , but he still knows the car.

“See you in a little bit. Just got to change.”

I watched as Jan pulled away. No sooner than I got into my apartment he pulled in front.

“Damn. Why can’t you let Jan see you too.”

I darted in and out of the shower. Sitting in front of my makeup mirror I felt his eyes stare through the window at me and a cold chill passed through my body like a cold winter snow.

I shook my hair and dressed in a hurry. The doorbell rang and Trevor pranced to the front and greeted Jan. Pulling the door open I peered around her body .

"Is he still there?" I asked.

She shook her head. "Damn " .

"Come on, let's go."

The evening air was damp from rain. I peered the streets waiting for Jan to unlock the car door.

"Damn it!" I screamed as I hopped in. "Just wish he would show his face. I'm starting to feel like a total idiot. You know, like a ghost following me or something, or as if I am in a dream. Oh, no nightmare."

"Come on, let's just go have some fun." said Jan. "Let's try that place you and Roman went to for something different."

Jan and I found a parking space quickly and raced to the door both looking like we needed a drink. We hesitated at the door, fluffed our hair, and laughed as we cooly walked in. The place was crowded, but we managed to squeeze into the bar and order a drink.

“Kind of looks like we intruded into a regular’s bar.” I whispered to Jan. “Yeah. Oh well. Just behave yourself Jan.”

“Hey, thanks.” she said sarcastically.

Jan and I edged ourselves down to the middle of the bar and stood joking about our fellow man making fools of themselves.

“Hey,ladies. What’s so funny?” a young, cute man interrupted.

“Just life.” I responded.

“Come here often?”

“Oh, come on get original.“ I looked at Jan in disbelief that this line still existed.

We sipped our drinks in synchrony. Our minds worked like clocks; both ticking in unison to get the next remark out.

“You girls go to Pitt?” he asked.

I looked around at the crowd and realized we must have been the oldest in the whole place.
“Why? Is that where everyone else here goes?”

He looked at both of us puzzled. “How old are you?”

“How old do you think we are? “ we questioned.

“Early twenties at least I guess.“ he suggested.

“Ok, thanks!”

“You two partying hardy tonight?” he asked.

“Nope. This is normal. Just a few drinks.” Jan responded.

“Well , we could…” he stopped and glared at us.

I looked at Jan’s watch for the time. Ten thirty.

“Want to go somewhere else?” she asked. Her eyes got big as I watched her expression of “ let’s get out of here”.

“Hey, where are you going? Want to go to my place? Just down the street.” the man shouted at us.

“No thanks.” we both replied as we ran to the car and laughed at our friends' actions.

“Let’s go to Ryan’s Pub before he follows us. God, what an asshole. “

“Was kind of cute until he opened his mouth.“ Jan laughed.

We luckily found a space around the corner, walked in, and found a vacant table. I ordered our drinks while Jan headed for the ladies room. The place was sparsely filled. As Jan arrived back, I took my run. Walking back to return to our table, I saw our friend had found us.

“Excuse me, that’s my chair.” I said .

He rose and pulled up a chair between us. Jan and I looked at each other in disgust, but figured it was something to amuse us for the time.

"Jan, it's quarter to twelve, better get going after these". I said.

"Oh. Didn't know it was that late. "Ok."

"Hey do you want to party some more?" he said in a drunken stupor.

Now here was a man or boy shall we say, that couldn't even stand without swaying to the breeze, very interested in both of us even though he probably couldn't even see us any longer. Wanting us to party? BIG FUN?!!?

"I've got to meet someone at the stroke of midnight and Jan probably has had enough of you."

"Well I can call you." he looked at Jan.
"Tell you what. Why don't you write your number down and we will call you."

He slipped a pen and paper from his pocket and eagerly gave us his number placing it on the table.

“You will call me won’t you?” he slurred.

“Yeah. Right.” we both said smiling and walking towards the door.

Jan mimicked laughing. “You will call me, won’t you?”

“It’s after twelve Ellen. Roman will be waiting.”

“He can wait for me. If he doesn’t, well…”

We pulled up in front of my apartment. Then reality set in ,my fear of night. We were both silent.
“Walk you home date.” Jan giggled.

“Okay.” I giggled as Jan grasped her umbrella.
“Expecting rain?”

“No. Are you expecting to blast someone out with your screamer? I looked down at my hand and automatically drew the little alarm to ward off attackers. Peter had given this to me . Probably because he knew I would be alone. Yes he knew.

“You know Jan.” I said staring at my hand, ”Never thought I’d depend on this little thing.”

“Just don’t blast that hunk waiting to open your door.” Jan whispered.

I looked up and saw Roman smiling at the car window. My eyes gleamed as I unlocked the door and let Prince Charming lead me out. I turned my head and winked at Jan.

Jan and I stumbled out of the car. Jan, still fisting her umbrella. Roman laughed as he led us both into the apartment.

“Just need to use the little girl’s room and say hello to Trevor.” Jan smiled.

Roman sat on the couch with me .

“Think you two are a little intoxicated. Never saw Jan like this. She’s funny.”

“Have a good time?“ he asked.

“Yeah, you know, a different good time. A girls night out good time.”

Roman hugged me and kissed me breaking off when Jan re entered the room.

“I’ll let you two alone.“

“That’s okay Jan. Sit down.”

“Come on Jan.” Roman coaxed. I made a drink for you too.”

“So, who tried to pick you up?“ he smiled. ”Everyone?”

Jan told him our adventures with all her humor. Roman’s laughter and smile filled the room as he sipped his drink. My eyes became glued to his smile until he met my attention. Jan noticed and said her goodbyes.

Roman romantically maneuvered me to bed, but my mind somehow was somewhere else tonight. I kept hearing echoes of a voice, a past voice. I thought it would go away, but tonight it would not dissipate. Near me, in the bedroom, holding me.

“What’s wrong?” he asked.

I couldn’t tell Roman. I couldn’t tell Roman that my thoughts were of someone else, were somewhere else.

Roman, after many hugs, left that night. I awoke, cried myself to sleep, hoping everything of Peter would disappear.

Chapter 53

I woke up with a better perspective, but feeling as if "yes this is it", I won't ever hear from Roman again. I didn't that day.

Saturday's workout was good,extra good. A lot of frustration dissipated. I told myself that I had to get moving, to get going, get up off your ass. Pack. The day went fast, and the evening came too soon. The phone started ringing it's familiar song.The phone rang and rang . Each time the recorder played the same message of laughter and hang ups.I listened as if I heard that song over and over, oblivious to the words. Grabbing the receiver in one hand, dialing Jan's number, I furiously packed.

"Jan, I can't take this much longer. "

"What are you doing?" she asked listening to the crunching of paper.

"Packing, listening to this damn phone ring, the doorbell ringing, Trevor barking from window to window and door."

"Don't answer the door. We'll find out who is playing these games. I'm coming over."

“Jan, that’s dangerous. “

“I got my weapons, don’t worry. Let’s see if we can catch at least a glimpse. I’ll ring your door twice at 12 noon.”

“Got it. Okay.”

As we hung up I shook my head. What weapons? Packing box after box, room to room with no semblance of order, I ignored phones, laughing voices ,doorbells and barks, but kept one eye on the clock wondering if Jan was out there yet. All of a sudden it stopped. There was a silence that scared me. I listened intently, but nothing. It felt like the merry go round stopped. No more revolving, no laughter, no music, no ringing bells. No nothing. It just stopped and left me sitting on a mid air pony.

The door chimes startled me. I listened to one, two,and then silence. Glancing at the clock’s hands pointing to 12:15 I read the signal Jan assigned, and rushed to the door to let her in.

"You know I was out there for an hour and didn't see anyone. Did you get any more phone calls?" she babbled.

I looked at her side, at a small baseball bat. Not answering I burst into laughter.

"Is that your weapon?" I laughed hysterically.

"Hey, don't laugh." we walked inside, Jan still grasping the mini bat.

"Let's see that. My God, what were you going to do with that?"

"You'd be amazed at what this can do." She swung the bat to and fro in her hand.

"Sorry, Jan." I smirked.

The last call I got was around 11:30.

"Damn, they have to slip up somewhere . They must have seen me. I don't know. " she said, still holding the bat.

"I don't know, but that's cute." I pointed to her bat again and laughed.

“Want me to take more boxes over while I am here? You sure are cleaning up fast Ellen.”

“You mind taking some of my important stuff with you?”

“VCR. Stereo?“

“No. I still need my music for my sanity. I know it’s only a couple more days, but I will wait to take it. My sister and husband are coming over to get some of the big stuff.”

“Okay. Call you when I get up.“

“Thanks Jan. I’ll carry it out to your car. ”God I can’t wait to get out of here.“

I watched Jan pack up and drive off.

Pick up, laughter. Pick up, laughter. I made myself a drink, a strong one, and opened an empty box. Staring at each empty corner I threw my favorite blue, holey blanket in and sat back fixing the satin edges smooth. My eyes became cloudy with tears. I probably shouldn’t have kept my mind up rationalizing, but damn, it bothered me. Here I was in this romance with Roman that was ending and it didn't hurt. I didn't have that reaction! That horrible sick feeling of over,gone! On one side, I felt fantastically strong and on the other, wondered if I would ever feel that deeply again as I once did. I changed channels and fell asleep.

Chapter 54

I felt Trevor's paw on my hand pulling me awake. The sun's rays brightened the room through the curtains and I hurriedly rushed to the window to see it's brilliance.

"Come on guy! Let's go!" I shouted to Trevor as I let him out back. I sat in the kitchen watching him enjoy the fresh morning summer air. I never believed what mental stability an animal could bring to someone's life, but now, yes I did. He was always there beside me, to listen, to share the good times and bad, and laughter and tears. He was there. Maybe even better than a human, I thought. Oh, yes,better. I knew if he left, it would be my own damn fault.

By the time I showered and dressed, Jan phoned with a" will be over in a bit message". It was gorgeous outside, perfect sun weather. I started loading my car with boxes upon boxes and smiled as my apartment became emptier.

"Looks like…" A voice from behind startled me and I turned swiftly with my arm held out in defense. I looked at Jan's face squarely as she stopped my arm.

"Jesus! Don't ever do that to me again." I began to reprimand. "You know I am a basket case, I am."

Jan grabbed my arm and led me into the house. She looked around.

"A little more and you will be out of here. Let's just take one load over and then we'll hit the sun."

"Yeah, got to keep my tan. I got to look good even if I'm a total mess. I'm sure there is going to be a rainy, gloomy day this week to do this stuff. Boy, John is sure going to be surprised when he sees how much I got done."

"Why do you say that Ellen?"

"Oh, you know men. Just don't think you can do things for yourself. Like you're going to break if you lift a box."

Jan rolled her eyes. "Let's go. Just follow me."

"Yep. Let's rev up those old motors and get the hell out of here." I laughed.

I followed Jan out a different route as usual. She was good at playing this mystery game, but I was getting familiar with my new territory. This time the road was a little rough. "Damn it!" I screamed as a box slid on my shoulder. With one hand driving and the other holding the box, we made it to our new home and I pulled up behind Jan.

"You know this moving can be hazardous. I almost had my arm amputated by a sliding box." I wittedly said to Jan. She just giggled.

As I entered the house and saw my boxes piling up, I looked out the window and grinned ear to ear. Jan looked at me strangely and smiled.

"Happy?"

"Hey, I finally did it, finally I'm so ecstatic I just can't tell you. Just can't wait to finally get everything here. Trevor, of course."

"I'm really glad for you," she said exhaustedly.

"Hey, we've got to get our paychecks at work. You ready?"

I pinched my cheeks and fluffed my hair.

"Ready now. Let's go. Don't have time to waste."

We flew to our office to retrieve our pay and then off to the bank for fun money.

"God, I look like hell. Oh, well. What can I say, working hard as usual." I joked. With the music jacked up to the max, and songs humming in our minds, we laughed at the working world and screamed out the window. "Hey we are having fun! Big fun!"

Stares and smiles reflected back upon my comment. The weather was chilly even though it was a late June day. We pulled in the front driveway and saw the guard sitting, nodding his approval.

"Ready. Let's go. I only expect to spend five seconds here so we can move on to the fun part of the day."

Jan laughed. “You have fun with or without money. You’ve certainly taught me to make my own good time.”

“Right Jan. Big fun, huh. Cops, robbers, thieves and derelicts. Big fun!”

We entered the front door and greeted the security guard.
“Hi Ray.“

“Hey ladies. How’s the vacation?”
“So far, good times.”

As the elevator opened and shuttled us to the fifth floor, I thought,” My God, I am a wreck. What a mess.” Hope Roman is not around”. Low and behold who stopped us first.

“Hey” he stopped. Wow,you really look scungy”. He said looking at me.

“Pardon me sir, I look what?” What the hell do you expect I’m trying to...“ my voice dropped, “ trying to get the hell out of there.

“Okay, don’t reprimand me, but ..” he whispered, “you look scungy.”

I backed out gracefully I thought. Scungy echoed in my mind. What nerve! What should I be wearing? Asshole! I exclaimed holding my breath.

“Hey.” Jan alerted me from my thoughts. I looked up like an alarm had gone off.

“Just aggravated by Roman’s comment. Scungy.“

We looked at each other and laughed in unison and said, “ Excuse me. I forgot to wear my evening gown. Men. God. They want you to perfect every minute no matter what you have to do. Sorry guys, yes I sweat too. We retrieved our paychecks and practically ran out to the car.

“Thanks, Ray.” He smiled and waved.

“You two look like you’re having fun. Anything going on?”

“All the time.” we announced.

The day became dismal, cloudy, rainy, and I was happy that one day was, just for my taking care of business purposes. My new home. Jan dropped me off at my apartment and I was glad to just get there and rest. Just for a moment.

"Ellen, I have plans tonight,but if you need me just call."

"I'll be fine, don't worry. Roman said something about coming over tonight."

Roman's comment penetrated my mind. I glanced in the mirror and looked at myself. You really do look bad. Really, as Roman said "scungy". From that day, I promised myself I would never go out looking that way. Without being myself. No, never go out without looking, without being my best. "Agree". I said in the mirror. And I muddled back agreeing.

Chapter 55

The day was almost near. Moving day. Moving out day. I had the day and the evening to myself. I was so excited to get away and leave my past behind. Sometimes I scolded myself for trying to run away, but never blinked an eye at the possibilities I had for a fresh new start. I called my sister, Julie to confirm they were still on for the move.

“Hey, Julie. Is Dave still….” She stopped me. “Yes of course. What do you have left? “

“Well, just the big stuff, but some little things to get me through the night.”

“Ok. Your friend is still helping out?”

“Oh.I forgot to call John. I’ll talk to you tomorrow. Should be ok.”

“See ya.” she signed off.

I quickly dialed John’s number hoping I wouldn’t get his infamous answering machine voice.

“Hello!” I bellowed as soon as I heard the receiver picked up by human hands.

"Hello Ellen. Gee ma tez, what's wrong?" he panicked.

"Oh, I forgot to remind you that tomorrow is the day. Can you still help me move or should I …"

John stopped me. "I remembered. Don't worry we are getting you on your way up and out." he joked.

"I'm so excited."

"I noticed. You didn't let me answer the phone. What time is this happening? What's left?"

"Well, still have the big stuff that's all.The waterbed."

"Did you syphon the water out?"

"Oh boy. That's a story in itself."

John laughed his crazy laugh. "What did you do to it?"

"Actually nothing yet, except I got the hose out."

"All you have to do is connect it to the bed and …"

"Look, John. I'm not stupid, but it's just a little difficult to get the water started, but I'll try."

"Ok." he laughed. "See you at, around eight? Is that ok?"

"Good. Great. "

"Hey, get some sleep. You'll need it tomorrow. "
"Oh, alright John."

I hung up and nodded to myself. Right sleep. I'm so excited I can't see straight, but the way I've been packing it really didn't matter. Each box contained a potpourri of things from this closet and that closet. No semblance of order. The only thing that mattered to me at this point was gathering my life and moving on. I continued packing and cleaning and trying to practically push everything out the door at this point.

Rrg!.

I stopped abruptly, tape still in hand to secure the last box as I glared at the phone. No, I pleaded. God no. Make them go away. Just for a moment. I thought I would go crazy if I heard that laughter one more time. But like a fool I grasped the receiver and picked it up.

Not speaking I held the receiver to my ear and froze, numb to any sounds of reality.

I heard a voice. " Ellen? Ellen? "

I shook myself to reality hearing my mother's voice. I wasn't sure as to how to explain to her that I could not tell her where I was, what the new number was, what the secret was all about and why. The why was something I could not explain to myself, let alone anyone else.

"Hi Mom. I'm sorry. Just trying to get everything done for tomorrow and my mind is not here."

"Are you alright? Julie and Dave coming over tomorrow to help? Not going to tell me anything more are you?" she rambled.

"Mom, just can't right now. I won't have a phone for a while. Just leave it at that for right now, okay? Love you."

“Me too.” she responded. “I will talk to you soon. Be careful.”

“Yep, always. That’s for sure.”

Tomorrow couldn’t come any sooner. It felt like days, but finally it was near. My day. I was excited and scared all rolled into one.

Chapter 56

Everything was arranged. Phone disconnected, gas off, electric off. Old ones off, new ones on. Goodbye Mifflin Street, Hello West Street. I watched with bated breath by the front window to see Dave’s truck pull up. Watching the clock impatiently, I jumped up and ran outside opening my sister’s door before they had stopped the engine. The sun hit the roof of the truck and reflected into my eyes. Partially blinded, I could still see Dave's face grinning and questioning, “What all has to go?”

“Well, come on in and see. Jan and I did a damn good job of getting everything out. Bed needs emptied though.”

“Come on let’s get that started.” he yammered.

Dave was always the go getter type. Let’s go, let’s get it done and let’s do it now. I always loved that about Dave and was proud to have him as my brother in law. My sister was very lucky with her marriage I always thought.

As soon as Dave entered the apartment he was moving. The hose was placed in the bed and water poured out into the street drain.

“Hey,” I yelled. “How did you do that so fast?”

“You probably just don’t have what it takes. “ he laughed.
“Well, I tried, but that hose wasn’t that hot to suck on !”

Just as that comment slid out of my mouth John walked in the door laughing.

“I won’t even ask what’s going on in here.”

Dave yelled out. “Is that the help?”

John introduced himself as usual and struck up a conversation. Suddenly, Jan flew in the door.

“Let’s go guys and get this stuff out of here.“

Little by little, the truck got loaded and the water bed emptied. As I walked out the door I heard a loud thump and laughter from the bedroom. I ran and gazed upon Julie and Jan stuck on the sinking waterbed mattress. They looked like two turtles on their backs, legs extended and struggling. Tears rolled from my eyes in laughter at the sight.

Dave and John walked in amazed and amused. "What's going on? Can we join?" we all laughed.

Julie and Jan rolled continuously on the bed forcing the water out.

The place emptied out. The guys had started to leave and John ran back in.

He looked at me. "Ellen, lock this door. See anyone around?"

"Really haven't looked to be honest, but I'll check it out."

John nodded and left with Dave. For once I hadn't even thought about this whole bizarre situation.

"Ellen. Are you okay"? What's going on?" Julie asked.

I looked at the floor. "I don't know, just don't know what is going on, but.."

Jan interrupted. "We've got to get her out of here. People are nuts. There is no reason to do the things they do anymore."

"I don't want to think about that right now. I've got to worry about getting over there and back by eleven, and getting John, out of here."

"Why?" they both exclaimed puzzled.

"I have a date at eleven." I said meekly.

"You've got what!" my sister laughed. "Looks like a great place to entertain now!"

I giggled as I pointed to each item in the living room. "Blanket, music", I said as I tapped the radio, and I opened my purse and pulled two wine glasses out, "and a little of the finest wine that he's providing."

"Sounds like Roman is coming over." Jan said.

"I can't believe you." Julie said, shaking her head and smiling. As I clinked the glasses together and smiled, we heard John and Dave talking and knocking on the door.

I grabbed my purse and stuffed the glasses back in yelling at the door. "Be right there!"

"Hey, it sounds like you guys are having fun in here." they inquired.

"Oh no. I am just entertaining again." I smirked. "So how did it go unloading over there?" I asked Dave.

"We had to leave the desk on the porch. Couldn't get it through the doorway for now. But okay. Should be one more load."

"It's getting dark out." I started worrying.

"It's only 8:30." John said looking at his watch.

"Yeah, well I got to.... " I stopped. "Dave has to go to work tomorrow and..."

I looked at Julie and Jan and they smiled. The last load got packed quickly and we decided to take my car. Julie and Dave would leave from there, and I would bring John back to his car at the apartment. John thought I would bring him back to my apartment and he would stay awhile, but I did have other plans.

Last load packed back and forth, back and forth and finally. Ahh. I stood in the middle of the living room and glanced around. Not teary eyed, but with thoughts of past memories.

John grabbed my shoulders from behind."Oh John." I said, my voice shaking.

"Ellen, it's okay if you want to…." I turned suddenly and laughed. No tears as John expected.

"You brat! " he exclaimed and laughed.

"No John. Just keeping the good memories. Can't be sad about good things can I now?"

"That's what I like about you. Always a surprise."

"Let's go Dave." Julie said edging Dave to the door knowing my deadline.

Like a caravan we paraded out. Reaching our destination, the new home, I asked John minute by minute, "What time is it?" Time was of the essence. I was ecstatic when the last load was completed. I walked Julie and Dave to the truck, hugging both with gratitude and watched as they pulled away.

"Want to drive my car John. I'm tired." He looked at me speechless.

You would have thought I offered John the world. As I climbed into the passenger side I looked at him.

"You know, not many are allowed the privilege to wreck my car."

John smirked as we pulled out and headed across the bridge. John's smile beamed.

"What time is anyhow John?"

He glanced at his watch. "10:15. Why?"

"Just tired. Want to go take a shower and go to bed."

"You want me to stay?"

"No! I'm good."

We arrived at the door and I thanked John endlessly for his help and hugged him.

"Call you tomorrow." he said.

"Ok." I nodded.

As I shut the door and looked at the clock I thought, "Shit. 10:30."

I ran to the shower and made a drink to slow down my nerves. I couldn't believe I was doing this. Having company at 11:00 again. Hair half dry and just a silk robe wrapped around me, I heard the doorbell ring. On time, dear lord. I looked in the mirror. Oh, not bad. I ran to the vestibule and saw Roman's face and smiled. He smiled back. As I opened the door I scurried back inside.

"Sorry," I whispered. "Just got back and a little damp but.."

He grabbed me in his arms and kissed me gently.

"You look sexy. Great."

"Hey, let me finish drying my hair okay?"

He went into the livingroom and I continued in the bathroom talking.

“All done. Just bare necessities.”

“We can have a picnic. Pretend it’s the baseball field.” he smiled.

“Radio.”

I walked into the living room doorway as he continued.

“Breeze.” as he turned the fan on high, and started spreading the comforter on the floor. Halfway through he looked up.

“Want to help me.” as he poured two glassed of wine from one hand. I grasped the comforter and smoothed the edges as Roman dimmed the light and layed down next to me leaning on one elbow. He handed me my glass, and then held his glass next to mine.

“You know.” he hesitated. His expression was solemn. My eyes looked at him in anticipation.

“We’ve had a lot of good times.”

“None have been bad at least.. “ I stopped.

He didn’t question me, only smiled.

“You’re one fantastic lady.” He hit his glass against mine. “Hope everything works out for you. To your new place.”

“Thanks Roman. Thanks for..” he put his finger to my lips, pulled me down next to him and whispered. “Not necessary.”

I smiled speechless. No words were necessary. We made passionate love on the picnic grounds of my soon to be old apartment, old home.

The apartment and Roman were extremely hot. Sweat poured from his body onto mine and I wiped the sweat from his brow. As I leaned over him I thought to myself. His eyes shut and resting. Glancing at the empty walls I smiled at all the good times Peter and I had in this place. All the good times. My tears had wiped them clean of anger of waiting for him to come over, of the pain I had gone through, and back and back again. And I finally realized all that was left was the joy and love he inflicted upon me. Roman pulled his arm around me and hugged me.

“Better let you get some sleep and I need the same.”

I layed on the comforter and watched as he dressed. Standing above me he pulled me up and kissed me goodnight.

“See ya.“

“See ya.”

I layed down with Trevor beside me wondering what it would be like if Roman would not be around, if John was not there. Would I go through all these traumatic experiences the same alone. Are they only just stepping stones in my life; only there to let the true colors of me spark; ignite and show the world this is Ellen. I fell asleep with my thoughts only to awake with music echoing on the bare walls.

Chapter 57

My last night. My last morning getting ready for work at this place and I was so excited. Tonight was my new home, my new world starting. It felt great! Jan pulled up out front and I ran to the car.

“Well you certainly have a smile on your face.” she grinned.

“This is it Jan. I can’t wait, that's all.“

“Well it is almost over. I’ll help you after work getting Trevor in and the rest of you.”

“Thanks, Jan. You don’t know what this means to me.”

“Oh, I have a good idea.”

Work was a breeze, no problems. Of course my mood was in the clouds. I slid to the side phone in the corner at work to call the P-force to inform them that “this was it, the big move.”

“Hi, this is Ellen.”

“You okay?”

“Yes. At work and just wanted to let you know that this was it. I will be at my new residence tonight. Anything you have to tell me now?”

“Well, we do have some ideas, but they are still vague right now. We’ll be watching.”

“Yeah, great, but I..”

“We will let you know. These things take ..”

“I know. Time. What else have I got? Thanks.”

I ran back to Jan to see if we were set for after work, but was interceded by Roman.

“Hey, how’s it going?”

“Alright. Going fine.”

“Call you later?”

“Yeah good.”

Halfway down the hall I stopped short and turned abruptly. Roman looked at me inquisitively.

I walked back to him writing on my notebook and tearing the corner off. As I reached him and looked into his eyes I handed him the piece of paper with my new number.

“Won’t do much good without this. Remember I changed.“ I stared at his face and he looked up smiling.

“Thanks” he winked. “Later.” He faded into the doorway and I turned to walk down the hall.

“Hey.” he popped backout.

“Free for lunch. I promised Deb and if you would..” That smile warmed me.

“Yes, I’d like. Meet you twelvish.”

Deb, Dr. Wright’s secretary, was standing and observing at the end of the hallway.

“You coming to lunch Ellen?” she asked.

“Yeah, Roman owes me lunch.” I looked at Jan’s face with a “oh no look”.

“Couldn’t say no to a free lunch, Jan.” I winked.

Jan smiled back as Deb walked back to her office.

"Be careful. Should be interesting, huh."

"Gotcha."

We all knew Deb by now. Where there is gossip, there is Deb. I let Jan know that I called my friends, the P-force, to inform them of the move. Just then Deb popped her head around the corner.

"You two have plans for the weekend. Where are you going?"

That was Deb! Always around the corner to find out what's going on in someone else's life. Inquisitive? No. Just downright nebby, gossipy. If there was something to know, she would be the first to know, or thought she knew. Somehow she knew my life had not been dull since the beginning of the year and she was dying to know what, who and when. That is why Jan had said to be careful. I loved keeping my secrets to myself and damn it bothered her. This was her chance at lunch to get her questions in.

Noon rolled around so fast I lost time. Looking at my watch, I grabbed my purse and ran out the door.

“God, five after. I’m late. See you guys in a bit. “I echoed to my staff as I rushed out the door.

My hyperness did not phase them. They were used to it by now. Deb and Roman stood in the hallway. Roman looked at me and pointed to his watch.

“Late. Huh,what’s this?”

“Excuse me. Some of us have to work for a living.” I sarcastically announced.

As we headed for the restaurant, Deb spoke.

“So why does Roman owe you lunch?”

I didn’t hesitate, and the words rolled from my mouth.
“Just some favors I did for him in PT.”

Roman brushed his arm against mine as if to say “good going”, she’ll accept that. I could tell he wanted to laugh, but held back. We approached the restaurant and were seated quickly.I felt a bit awkward, especially when Roman started playing games under the table. We ordered immediately. Deb ordered Italian pasta and I ordered the house salad with house dressing. Deb and Roman looked my way as I ordered.

“Is that all you are ordering?” Deb questioned. “Boy, that’s being easy on Roman’s budget. Kind of a boring lunch too.”

“Oh.” Roman interrupted.”So that’s how you keep so slender.” he said as he ran his leg down mine.

“Just not into food that much, Deb. I’d fall asleep at work if I ate lunch like you do.“

Roman smirked. “Well we know what Deb does in her office after lunch now.”

Deb never scrimped on someone else’s budget, only her own. As lunch was served, Deb looked at me.

“So where are you living?”

“An apartment right now in the Swissvale area.”

“You moving?” she questioned again.

“Thinking of it.”

“Your place...” Roman started staring into my eyes. I kicked him under the table. His eyes were surprised.

“Near Regent Square?” he added.

“Yes, it is.“ I responded.

I knew Roman was about to say something that Deb’s gossipping mind could feed on. Roman knew what my reaction meant. Stop. Think of who you are giving information to. I could tell Deb did not like the shortness of the conversation. The rest of the lunch was utter chit chat and as we wrapped it up, Roman paid the tab, and we both thanked him graciously. He walked us both back to work. Deb had walked down the hallway and turned back to Roman.

“Thanks again.”

He smiled and looked at me whispering, “See you later.”

I smiled as I walked back to the office and kept that smile the rest of the day.“

"Oh, Friday. Five oclock." I was so excited.

New life! New home!

Jan and I met in the hallway and grinned at each other. As we took the elevator and I opened the front door to leave work, it felt like I had opened Pandora's box. I opened my eyes and the sun shone and I saw a trillion butterflies gliding towards the heavens.

"Free. Free at last " I whispered under my breath.
"I'll be over as soon as I change." Jan said.

I ran into my apartment and greeted Trevor. "This is it kid. We are out of here." I hurriedly changed into comfy clothes and started packing the remains. Before Jan had a chance to ring the doorbell, I had everything ready to go. Just basic clean up now. Jan scurried and took things to the car and looked at me.

"That's it. Just Trevor." she stated.

We checked around the apartment looking in every cupboard and we both ended up in the middle of the echoing kitchen, face to face.

"This is it!" I yelled with relief in my voice. Shutting my eyes, one tear welled in my right eye.

Jan looked at me.

"Only one tear of joy, that's it. Only good memories. That's all that is coming with me. Let's go!"

I grabbed Trevor's leash and as I grabbed the doorknob, I glanced around the room one more time. Slowly shutting the door I sighed deeply and grinned.

Trevor layed down peacefully on the front seat. I looked down and petted his brows.

"I promised you a house and I never break my promises."

Chapter 58

Following Jan, we made it to our new home in little time and parked behind the house. Jan and I simultaneously got out of our cars and Trevor jumped out with joy.

“Hey Jan. “How does it feel to have new neighbors?”

She smiled and started talking to Trevor.

“Come on Trevor. Let’s go see your new home.”

As we reached the front door I glanced side to side, just to make sure no one was around. I was always paranoid, or was it cautious. I couldn’t determine any difference amongst the two anymore. I opened the door and felt home, peace and instant satisfaction within myself. I finally got a home. Trevor sniffed at every corner and finally after nosing one of our unpacked boxes, mellowed down beside it and half closed his eyes.

“I guess I got approval?”

“I think you got the okay from the kid.” Jan smiled. “Well, I’m going to let you guys settle in.”

“What time do you have Jan. I forgot Roman is coming over.”

“It’s about 9:30.

“Oh gee. He’s probably on his way and I’m a wreck.”

“Ellen. You look great. Remember what you always say to me. Fluff your hair, pinch your cheeks and look great.”

I laughed.

“I did tell you that Jan, but it doesn’t always work. Especially when the guy that’s coming over always looks perfect. It’s disgusting.”

Jan rolled her eyes. “Must see perfection in someone else to be coming around.“

I smiled halfway. I was still confused by the whole situation, but loving every moment. I rushed up the stairs and somehow managed to look put together in twenty minutes. I hesitated in the bathroom mirror tracing my mouth with my fingertip thinking of how I had grown and molded myself from a fruppy, just rolled out of bed gal to a glowing painted fingertips woman. I heard the chimes of the doorbell and smiled at the top of the stairway. Trevor was barking and prancing at the screen door of our new home. Roman's voice whispered, "Trevor, where's mom?"

Making my way down the stairs in between unpacked boxes, our two smiles joined as I opened the door. Roman's eyes roamed around the living room as he grabbed me in a big bear hug.

"Wow!" he drew from his mouth as his eyes centered back to me.

"That's for both. This place is great and you look fabulous. Show me your place. Looks great so far."

I pulled at Roman's arm from room to room, and up the stairs smiling proudly.

"How did you get all of this stuff in your old apartment?"

I laughed at him. "I don't know, but where there is a will ,there is definitely a way."

Roman sat down on a pile of boxes and pulled me on his knee.

“You happy? Is it all ok now?”

“Yes, Roman. I am extremely happy, but nothing is ever over until you finish it.”

I never saw a man get so involved in my words. He seemed to analyze each one and take the wisdom (as I always said, of an older woman), home each time with him.

“I’ve learned alot from you,” he said.

“What do you mean?”

“Most of the girls, women I know, aren’t like you. I’ve learned that there is a different feeling for a true woman. Like we have. No questions. No pressure. Just a true good feeling of enjoying each other’s company.”

Roman flashed his perfect smile and kissed my hair.

I could have said so much at that time, but I didn’t. I just smiled back. Bouncing me up from his knee he yelled.

“Hey, I came over to help you. What can I do?”

I thought for a moment and said, “ Stereo? Can you help? I need my music.”

Eagerly he grabbed my arm and piggy backed me down the stairs. We waded through the boxes and he started to work. I left him and wandered into the kitchen to bring out the bottle of wine. As soon as I opened the bottle I panicked. Glasses? The cupboards are still bare. I then spotted my infamous knapsack and remembered that last evening in the apartment. “Great!” I said to myself as I pulled the two out. As I started to pour I heard music generating through the rooms. Gracefully dancing in the room I handed Roman his glass as he smiled contently above the stereo.

“Stereo works.” he grinned, grasping his glass and motioning to me to sit beside him on the couch. He lifted his glass and I in turn.

“To you. To happiness always.“ We sipped our wine and Roman pulled me atop his luscious body and kissed me. He stopped short.

"A million dollars could not replace this friendship."

"I feel like a million dollars. Even if I had it, what could I even buy with it that would compare to what we have; what you have meant to me in my life right now."

Roman shut his eyes and hugged me so that I could hardly breath, let alone speak.

But no words were necessary. My thoughts were enough to satisfy the world. Roman did not know what effect he had on my life at that time. Nor did I on his. How detrimental this whole innocent affair had on my personality and my life at this point. My life had turned from one negative disaster into everything coming up roses and sunshine. Before I knew it, it was time to close the evening again. Funny thing about us. We never ever said goodbye. The evening always ended with a "call you later", "see ya tomorrow", or so and so , or just a plain kiss, hug and prolonged glance into each other's eyes of “thank you”. Thanks for sharing a part of your life with me.

After Roman’s departure, Trevor and I curled on blankets on the only cleared part of the living room by the door. We listened to the strange new noises of our new home, but it did not deter either of us from a solemn night's sleep.

Chapter 59

We were awoken by the sunlight brilliantly shining through the doors windows. Trevor pranced beside me waiting to take his morning run outside. I abided by his request ,hugging him.
"Come on guy! Time to start a new day." I smiled enthusiastically more and more each day. I looked around as I headed towards the back door and realized my work was practically never ending for the day. Trevor came first. We went outside to the back yard. I looked at the clouds and realized it was not a "sun day." Trevor wandered the yard and then ran back following me indoors. Glancing at the clock, I rushed upstairs to make myself presentable for the day. One more last glance in the mirror, I proclaimed and nodded affirmative. Proceed. No matter what was going to happen today, a green light was ahead. Trevor looked up at me with the same expression. I raced him down the stairs to the kitchen. My first tackle of assembling my household life. Tugging at a packed box I opened it hastily. Trevor laid beside me with questioned

brows of "Are we staying?" I patted his head and he closed his eyes as if to say okay, I'm content.

Our peaceful household was interrupted by the phone echoing around each box. We both scurried to the doorway to answer.

"Hey! Morning! Jan sang.

"Hi Jan, you're up early."

"It's ten. Knew you would be up by now. Want some help?"

"Sure, this is a mess. John is coming over to paint the bedroom."

As soon as I spoke I saw his car pull up.

"Speak of the devil!"

"Oh, okay. I'll be over." I knew Jan was a John fan.

John and Jan arrived at the door at the same time. They both greeted me with smiles.

"Did you run over Jan?"

"Well, considering I am right next door it wasn't hard."

"So what's up?" John looked at the kitchen lined up with boxes rearing to find their new place in our home. He made his way upstairs without hesitation and started rearranging for his paint job. I ran up to see what he needed, but he was already hard at work. The warm air from the bedroom window blew gently and John smiled.

"I'll give you a holler if I need anything." he winked.

I ran back downstairs and saw Jan diligently unwrapping and putting glasses into the cupboard.

Immediately my temper flared. "Jan, no that's not what I want to do. Those cupboards need to…"

I stopped knowing that it was just my emotional state, the me wanting to do this, the, I'm on my own and I will make it on my own state of mind. The selfishness and distraught feeling of evasion. I tried to calm my nerves. Friends were not the people I wanted to hurt, but sometimes the anger is the easiest to let out to them or on them.

"Jan. I'm sorry."

Jan sat down. "Okay. Just let me know what I can do?"

I laughed. "There is actually nothing left for you to do. You've done enough."

"Bullshit! That's what friends are for."

"Stop it." I joked. "I'm so sick of that song."

Everytime Jan would reassure me with this phrase all I could hear was the tune of the year playing over and over again in my mind. As true as the lyrics were, it became, as most popular songs, redundant and boring after a while.

"Jan. Let's go bar hopping tonight !!" I surprisingly said.

"What?"

"You know, just kind of not be at one place too long. We'll confuse those assholes if they have any intentions of bothering me here."

"Sorry Ellen. But I have a date tonight." she announced smiling.

"Great Jan! Anyone I know?"

"No, not yet, or maybe not at all?" she smiled. "You know my luck."

"Good for you!"

"You be okay?"

"Yes. Perfect." I whispered.

"See ya. Have fun."

As Jan closed the door, John hollered down the stairs.

"Ellen, come look!"

I rushed up the stairs to see the beautifully painted eggshell white bedroom.

"Oh, John.Thank you. It looks fabulous."

I reached with open arms to hug John who was covered in paint. He hesitated and I smiled with a noddingly ok, I don't care look.

"You are welcome." he said softly. "Glad I could help, however I do have to run. I have family and work stuff I have to do tonight. Will you be ok?"

"Yes, we will be okay."

And John packed up and headed out. I watched as he walked down the stairs to his car and drove down the street. I suddenly felt alone. But not lonely.

Chapter 60

I poured myself a glass of the white Zinfandel that was left from the other night with Roman and sat down on the living room couch. Trevor sat at my feet and I gazed at nothing. Nothing at all. I thought of all the people who entered my life in the last few months. Smiling, I had no regrets or qualms of what was, or what was to be. I felt at peace. It's amazing how people come into your life and fade away, but the good memories stay.

I picked up the phone and dialed slowly as a voice answered.

"Hello. Peter." I said smiling. "How are you?"

"Ellen?" the voice echoed surprised.

"Yes it's me. Just wanted to know if you were free for maybe a few drinks and catching up?"

Made in the USA
Columbia, SC
15 November 2022

71061031R00224